The
NAKED
TRUTH...

THE JOURNEY
FROM WITHIN

Anthony L. Leslie Jr

This story is inspired by true events. A select few names and locations have been altered to protect the identity of others. If you contributed or supported in any fashion I thank you for being one vessel to help convey 'The Naked Truth the Journey from Within.' To my models thank you for bringing my words to life and thanks for assisting in separating this book from your average read.

ISBN: 1482641968
ISBN-13: 9781482641967

Dedication

To all the people stuck in a storm or going through a storm. People whose faith is growing weak and those who feel low. This is your validation! Be encouraged and lean on your own understanding. Remember, no sin is greater than any other sin. You don't have to take my word, just read the Bible.

To my beautiful mother Terry Snell thanks for assisting me on my walk to righteousness. Thanks for listening and teaching me how to survive. You are more than amazing; you are my *first love* and will forever be my number one girl.

My friend Mark Gentry, you calm my fears and make me feel loved. Your faith in me has uplifted me, thanks for sharing my truth. Were it not for all the questions you asked, the book would be incomplete.

To my eldest baby Robert Wellington, I need you just as much as you need me. Remember to accept people the way they are without judgment. Help and be considerate of others, and be certain to always praise GOD. You deserve the best because that is what you are and what you give.

My youngest boy Justin Gipson, no matter what anyone says, remember that you are a precious gift from GOD. Keep in mind that you are loved and part of me will always be with you, and I know part of you will always belong to me.

To my darling grandmothers, Marilyn Leslie and Barbara Snell, who take on many roles in my life, you are and will always be my true friends and my father figures. You have given me the greatest gift man can give: THE WORD OF GOD and it will forever be appreciated and cherished. From the depths of my soul I thank and Love you both.

Queen Annie Leslie, I could brag for days about you, but only GOD understands, that you are truly heaven-sent.

Anyone who bought read or supports me and my books, I can't thank you enough and I appreciate each of you. I won't forget you-all of whom make me better than I am.

Table of Contents

An Innocent Child of GOD

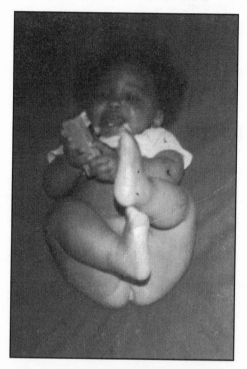

Baby Hippo, Tone

Forward

The Bible says: *We are all made equal* (2nd **Corinthians 8: 12-15, 1st Kings 8: 46, and also in the book of Isaiah 46: 5)** but life has a funny way of making us feel that they are just written words, and they fall on deaf ears. The Bible also says: *No sin is greater than any other sin, and we are all born sinners* (**Psalms 51: 5 and Romans 5: 12)**. We are all born imperfect human beings. Tell that to a victim of rape, a heroin addict, and a bisexual man. Although it's a known truth, some of us use the Scriptures as a scapegoat to justify our shortcomings, sins, and wrongdoings. I was taught right from wrong at a very young age. Although I find it hard to fly straight at times; sometimes I just want to spread my wings and just glide. I've been a lot of places, and I've seen a lot of things in my short life. I feel like I've seen it all and done it all. They say birds of a feather flock together. You may think like an eagle, but if it quacks like a duck and looks like a duck, nine times out of ten it is a duck. The upside of that cliché is GOD does allow U-turns, so it's up to you to decide if you want to be an eagle, a swan, a peacock, or just keep quacking like a duck the rest of your life.

Take a journey with a recovering addict who is struggling with his sexuality and in search of peace and balance in this chaotic thing called life. He's reminded that death is not an option. See how a man can be knocked down and get back up. See how others can make you challenge your beliefs and kill your dreams before you realize they exist. Watch how one man's faith is tested and questioned. Observe the power of influence that people around you possess and witness the growth of one man's spirituality. If truth is an attraction for you, you'll have a full understanding of the drug game's uncensored ugly truth; it will be fully exposed and revealed. You'll also come to understand the good, the bad, and the ugly part of the gay society, when one is a part of "The Life" (Gay Community).

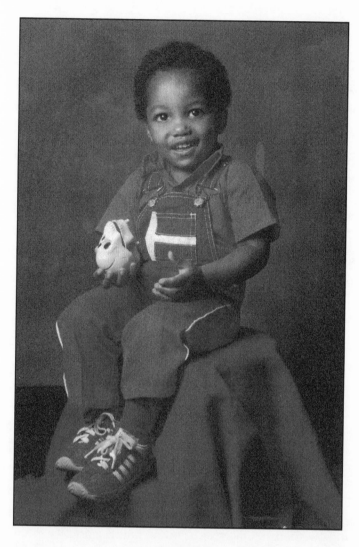

Tony Roni'

"Taz"   short 4 Tasmanian devil

Fatty, Millie and Bubby @ grannies
The Honey Comb Hideout

CHAPTER 1

The Naked Truth: The Unseen, The Unheard, And The Never Told

When I was six years old, my father was arrested for attempted murder on a police officer, which was one of many violations. My mom was a single mother, fresh out of her teens, never married, and she was determined to remain faithful to my dad while he was upstate doing a bid of twenty-five to life. Any possibility for a positive or consistent male role model was slim to none. I started to have my own Bible study every week with my soul mate, my maternal grandmother, Barbara, who was a baptized Jehovah's Witness for many years. I really enjoyed having my Bible studies and internalized all that positive information at a young age. I felt special, and I knew early that all our blessings come from above, and moms and dads whom we hold so dear could leave or be taken away, but GOD would never leave or forsake us.

I'm forever thankful for the biblical basis and foundation my grandmother Barbara (Mommy) gave me at an early age. I was blessed to pick up so many of her good characteristics in the process of learning about the Bible. I cherished people, family, friends, pets, stray dogs. You name it, I loved it. I just had a lot of love in my heart when I was young.

I was a momma's boy three times over. I was Granny's baby! Granny is Marilyn, my paternal grandmother. We have a special bond as well. I was like her last child, only in reality I was her grandbaby. I don't know what strengthened our bond so much, it was just strong. Anyone around could feel it or sense it. Most people just accepted it or were jealous of it. Granny birthed eight children and has so many grand and great-grandchildren. Some of my family couldn't understand me and Granny's relationship, but others could identify with a mother's love for her child. From the outside looking in, it's clear my life could be defined as broken, but the thing I was never without was love.

My favorite mammal is an elephant for so many different reasons, but the reason I love elephants most is we have similar characteristics and traits. Elephants have a long life line, with a photographic memory that lasts a lifetime. They are gentle animals and remain mild tempered until you set them off or pose a threat to them or their family. I like the idea that they have tough skin and stick close to their families. The thing highlighted in my mind most is that elephants have such a good memory, which leads me to open my book with some of the worst memories of my life. I buried these events so far in the back of mind I honestly believed at one point that they never happened. Not once, not twice, but three times I was a victim of sexual abuse, and to me no one act was less hurtful than the other.

The first time I was touched inappropriately was at the age of four years old. We were raised like cousins, but she was actually a friend of the family. We were all outside playing hide-and-go-seek, and Dianna and I hid under the porch together. After awhile we were still unnoticed, and she pulled my pants down and performed fellatio on me. I watched how she moved and how she touched me, and I couldn't believe how my body responded. I was so afraid I was going to get in trouble and someone would know we were doing something we were not supposed to. To our surprise Aunt Dora, an OG [old gangster], was on the porch and witnessed the whole act. Later we all addressed the issue: Dianna's mom, my mom (Terry), Dianna, Aunt Dora, and me. My mother was absolutely furious beyond measure. She was angry with Dianna's mother, Dianna, and me too, for that matter.

Luckily Aunt Dora came to my defense and saved me from a fierce ass whipping. She pleaded with Terry, "Don't be angry with Tony. He didn't do anything. He was just standing there and really didn't know what was going on."

Terry spat back at Aunt Dora, "His ass knows better, and if he didn't, he'll know the next time."

Today I can understand why my mom was so angry. I understand her anger toward Dianna and her mom and the whole situation. She didn't want her son corrupted or introduced to any sexual behaviors at four. Today I also understand Dianna's actions. She was raised in a house full of children, and they were all subjected to sexual abuse on a regular basis by their own grandfather. They had a live-in rapist and pedophile. Now it's clear to me we all have a story, and no matter how bad things are, I know that situations can always be worse.

It was quiet and the house was finally settled and calm after that eventful day. I lay in the bed, alone in my room, with the TV on mute. My room was dark, and the light from the TV beamed in the room with a blue-tint. I was restless and wanted nothing more than to fall asleep before my father came home. I imagined I was scheduled for a beating upon his arrival, and I assumed if I was asleep, it would save me from a beating. Later that night my dad, Anthony Sr., returned home along with my two uncles and his best friend, Kenny. The voices of my uncles and Kenny eased my fear because I knew my dad would be in good spirits with his company in tow. When they arrived home, my aunts came downstairs to greet the men and join the party, while my cousins tailed behind.

Like a pair of well trained monkey's my cousins came right in my room and questioned me, "Did your mother beat your butt?"

I replied sourly, "No."

We all knew that if she didn't, most likely my dad would have the honors. Moments later my dad called me into the living room.

I stood in the doorway, and he smiled and said, "What's up, Lil' Man?"

To my surprise all the men applauded my behavior: "Lil' Anthony Jr. getting his knob polished at four, Das my nigga."

My uncles and my dad's friend joked with Anthony Sr. and found humor in the situation.

When my mother walked in, the conversation came to a sudden end. She looked at my dad and said, "Don't encourage that shit."

Prior to my father going to jail, my grandmother Marilyn was the land-lord of our three-story detached house off of Liberty Heights and Gwynn Oak. Seven of us shared one household: Me, Anthony Sr. (my dad), Terry (my mom), Aunt Dora, Tamia Dora's daughter (who was two years my senior), Aunt Pat, and Warren (Pat's son, who was five years my senior). The first floor had two bedrooms, one bath, and a kitchen; the second floor had two bedrooms, one bath, and a kitchen; and, finally, the third floor had two bedrooms and one bath.

At the time Anthony Sr. was the head of the household. He owned two Good Humor ice cream trucks and was a big-time drug dealer; he was well respected in the drug game. Anthony Sr. was a good provider and a good dad, considering he was fairly young himself [children raising children— *imagine that*]. My dad was a very attractive guy. He had a slender build and weighed about 135 pounds. He was light brown–skinned, with dark brown beady eyes that exhibited danger and mischief. His ears were fairly large, but they looked perfect with his full face. Although he was the head of the house, everyone in the family unit would link up and try to do their part to maintain the household, raise the children, and, above all, have fun.

The home at 4211 Fernhill Avenue was indeed a party house; it had the food, drink, weed, drugs, and the guns. The house itself was well respected. When Anthony Sr. was arrested, that in turn forced the women to take on odd jobs; as retail clerks, waitresses, and stylists. They had to run the ice cream trucks, coupled with caring for the children. Although Tamia, Warren, and I were all first cousins, we were raised in the same household as brothers and sisters, and we treated one another as such.

One thing I think my dad, his sisters, and his brothers learned early was that one Leslie child was more than enough; they all had one child and called it quits. We were all an energetic bunch, full of fire, and always in something, and I wanted to fight the whole neighborhood, or at least I was encouraged to. Walking was a foreign concept to the Leslie children. Like most kids we had to run, flip, skip, and jump everywhere. One of my closest cousins was prescribed the prescription Ritalin before he hit his teens. The family suggested my mom should put me on a small dose as well, but as quiet and mild mannered as my mom was, she stood firm in that area. She simply said no and stuck to her guns. Several years passed and it was mentioned again, and Terry made it clear the subject was not up for discussion. She would reply, "He's hyper, but he'll grow out of it."

Another graphic, vulgar unpleasant incident still haunts me every time I think back on the conflict in my early childhood. I still have yet to create closure with the events that took place with Joey when I was a defenseless child. At about five years old my neighbor Ms. Jackie had a day care she ran from her home. Her house was located two doors down from my house. She had two sons, Joey, who was twelve years old, and Jamal, who was my age. Jamal was my best friend. He was the only child in the neighborhood that was my age, and we favored one another. We both were brown-skinned, with curly black hair; we had small, petite moms whose long, jet-black hair had that Indian effect. My dad and my mom fought when I was younger. My dad was in the habit of being in control, and my mom, on the other hand, was full of fire. Jamal was also subjected to a home with a mom and a stepdad who fought quite frequently. Only GOD knows what else Jamal had to go through being raised in a home full of secrets, chaos, and, above all, with a brother like Joey. Jamal and I played well together. We liked to act like we were brothers and spent a lot of time playing outside and visiting one another's homes.

One day I went over to Jamal's house like any ordinary day. I remember approaching Jamal's front door; the door was open, and the screen was closed and locked. It was very quiet and very dark inside. I looked inside and knocked softly on the door.

"Jamal," I called through the screen door.

Jamal's older brother came to the door. He was dark-skinned, husky, and big for his age, a giant to me at the time. Joey let me in and led me to the back of the house in the direction of Jamal's bedroom. Instead he took me straight to the bathroom. At this point I was alarmed, but this was a place I was familiar with, a place where I felt comfortable and safe.

Joey shut the door and said with his deep, mannish voice, "Let me see your thing."

I said, "No," and reached for the door.

He then picked me up and stood me on the toilet and asked me, "Are you scared of me?"

With my head held down in shame, I answered him in a low tone with a simple "no," but I knew I was afraid. I also knew it was wrong for me to show anyone my pee-wee.

I recall him saying, "I show Jamal my penis, and he shows me his all the time."

I said, "No, I don't want to."

He assured me if I didn't show him my private parts; he wouldn't allow me to see Jamal anymore. Losing your only best friend is a big deal to a five-year-old child. He then unzipped his zipper and pulled his pants down and fully exposed himself to me. I remember feeling not only afraid but ashamed and embarrassed. I was frozen completely still. Joey unbuttoned my belt, and I quickly grabbed my pants to stop him.

He told me, "I'm not going to touch it. Just let me see it." And then he moved my hands and opened my pants.

After Joey touched and fondled him and me simultaneously, he then told me to put his penis in my mouth. He removed his hand from my private area and grabbed me behind the neck. Then he had his way with me for a short while.

He pulled himself back and told me to suck it like a Blow Pop. He said, "Let me show you."

Joey put my penis in his mouth and commenced to show me how to suck.

After that day I never returned to my friend Jamal's house. I never shared the event with anyone.

I remember the second time Joey got me alone. He was riding his bike past my house, and I was on my front porch.

Joey asked my mother, "Can Tony ride to the store with me?"

At that very moment, telling was an option, but I dismissed that idea within seconds. I was afraid to speak, afraid of how Joey would react, and even afraid how my mom would react. Feeling embarrassed, once again I froze. I rode to Jacks, the local mini market in our neighborhood, on the back seat of Joey's bike. After stopping by Grove Park Elementary school yard, Joey verbally reminded me of exactly how he liked his blow pop licked. In the back of the school, what he did to me was hidden by the fence and guarded by trees. As time passed, I completely forgot about these events and erased them from my mind.

For several years I was free from being anyone's victim of sexual abuse, until I was approached one more time by my own flesh and blood. At just nine years old, I would be asleep and wake up to my male cousin humping on me through my clothes. I remember pretending to still be asleep, because I didn't know how to react. I recall on different occasions lying with my arms at my side, my hands tightly gripping the thick seem stitch around my waste while discreetly holding my pajama bottoms up.

One night my cousin started humping on me through my clothes again and suddenly decided to take a different approach. My cousin got frustrated, got up, and turned the light on.

He told me, "You're not sleep."

I continued to pretend to be asleep. He waited awhile and watched me; he then put a porn movie in the VCR and played with himself until he reached his climax. I don't know what event frightened me more at nine years old: the idea of being a human humping bag or the image I witnessed. One thing I knew for sure was that it was time to stand up for myself. These events with my cousin were few and far between because we were only around one another when we both visited Granny's house on the same weekend. Of course I was over at Granny's every weekend, but my cousin wasn't there as often as I was. We called Granny's house the Honeycomb Hide-Out.

One day Granny picked me up for the weekend, and she and I went to pick my cousin up in the inner city on Sticker Street. Granny sat in the car and honked the horn several times before she sent me up to the door to tell my older cousin to hurry up because Granny was waiting. The Front door was open, and I called out for my cousin as I ran straight upstairs toward my cousin's room. No one was in the bedroom, and the bathroom door was slightly ajar. I saw my cousin sitting on the edge of the tub, performing fellatio on his older half brother, who is of no relation to me. Memories of Joey resurfaced and took me back five years, and I ran out of the house as fast as I could. Now I truly understood the meaning of a snowball effect. I had gone into the house with the intent to tell my cousin to come on, then I wanted to race back to the car to claim the passenger seat for shotgun.

I remember thinking to myself before I went in the house, "I am going to run back to the car like my life depended on it," unaware that sometimes we speak things into existence.

Over the next few years I began to stand up to my older cousin and not allow him to hump on me. I no longer fell subject to the tactics of older deserves particular privilege syndrome, I no longer allowed him to make me wait on him or settle for second best because his age holds rank. I didn't fight my sleep until the wee hours of the night, afraid of what might happen. I welcomed his attempts; as a matter of fact, I couldn't wait to defend myself by any means necessary. We always had a competitive relationship: who could run the fastest, who was the video king, who could ball up the best, etc. When he came into my room, he and I had a real fist fight, like two strangers in the street. It was the first time we had ever fought to that extent. We woke the whole house up. We were on the third floor and ended up on the second floor. This night would determine our relationship in the near future.

I recall my grandmother and my favorite Aunt finally coming to the second floor to stop the fight. At this point I had calmed down. I was satisfied with the work I just put in on his ass. I took a seat to respect my grandmother, but my cousin, on the other hand, was now out of control, running his mouth, and still making threats. After enduring his verbal threats for a short while, I jumped up. I then grabbed a porcelain duck by the neck and used it to gash my cousin's head, cut him across his chest, and wound him on his right forearm.

I had been in many fights prior to this one, but usually in school or in the presence of an authority figure, someone to stop the fight once it progressed to the level where blood was drawn or any serious damage was done. My fights were usually quick and short: a couple hammers to my opponent's face and the game was over. I never kicked a man when he was down, and I always took pity on people, so once they got the message, I backed off.

This time was different. There was no one to attempt to break us up, and I was like an animal in a rage. I didn't want to stop until I saw blood. Even though my cousin and I fought a lot growing up, all the way until we reached our late teens, we still loved and defended each other in the streets. After that fight, I was sure that a good ass whipping could fix any problem. Fighting was always in my spirit, but a fight to this degree helped people understand words without speaking [no more mixed messages].

After that situation my cousin and I maintained a healthy and close relationship until his life was taken in 2005. He was shot in the back of his head in broad day light in the middle of the street in Baltimore city. That was ironic because at the time I was just building the strength to have a sit down and create closer with my cousin. I remember before he was mercilessly murdered my other cousin Tamia visited him in jail and told him that I was openly gay. At this juncture I had already shared with my family and friends several years ago, that I was a bisexual man. Unexpectedly my cousin Tamia came home and shared with me that he was upset and displeased with my decision to live an alternative lifestyle. I was absolutely appalled and shocked. That report motivated me to find time to have a one on one discussion with my older cousin. Many functions and family affairs had come and gone where we attended and enjoyed seeing one another; unfortunately we never got a chance to address the subject. It was never the appropriate time or place to concentrate on such a serious matter. More importantly we already developed a mutual love and respect for one another and we shared the secrets of our past.

Although I had some horrific immoral events and situations touch my life at an early age, I am blessed to be able to say I was never penetrated or taken advantage of to the fullest extent. Through it all, I learned to forgive and value people when they are here because life is short and unpredictable. I've learned that speaking up, and out is medicine for the soul! Secrets rob you of your peace and rents unwarranted space in your mind and heart. So feel free to free yourself, and be your complete authentic self because that alone is a force to reckon with. If you have a wound take the band-aid off and watch the healing process take its course. Many times the truth hurts, but in the end it can only produce good merit and may even help someone in the process.

Model

Kay-Kay and Anthony @ Prom

Anthony L. Leslie Jr.

CHAPTER 2

You Already Possess Everything You Need To Be Great

School was always enjoyable and an easy task for me. I was a very good student; school was a job that required very little effort. I was popular and always maintained a good rapport with my teachers. I was always a likable person and had a unique way of making people feel comfortable, secure, and safe, like I was a bodyguard or purely just a trusted friend. People felt important when they were in my company.

It always pleased me to make others feel good or valued. I could always bring a smile to someone's face. I have a rare talent for finding the good in any situation or person. I allow people to feel feelings most adults spend a lifetime trying to experience, even if it's only for a short while.

Although I liked school and had a desire to excel and please my mom and both my grandmothers by doing well, I frequently fought. Fighting was something I was good at and enjoyed doing as well. I was an only child and had a very short fuse. In school I had smooth, caramel-brown skin and charcoal-black hair that I wore tempered, and I didn't have a single hair on my face. With full lips and perfect white teeth, I stood five foot seven and weighed 140 pounds, which left people wondering how such a small-framed guy could be so dangerous. I was an attractive young man who dressed well and had a reputation for being a Tough Tony [go figure]. Many times people wanted to test my reputation to build their own reputation.

My mom didn't approve of my violent nature because she believed it was just a learned behavior, which I later found to be true. She wanted me to be her sweet, nice, respectful, and well-mannered son, and reveal qualities she knew dominated my character. My mom would tell me sometimes I was like Jekyll and Hyde, or a ticking bomb. I would be fine, and all of a sudden someone or something would just set me off. My family and friends loved to see me go off, and they would wait to see the action unfold. It was amusing and usually worked in their favor. People would say, "Oh, we got a beef, call Tony." And nine times out of ten, their beef would instantly become just my beef. I would get in trouble for fighting someone else's battle. In my mind I wasn't doing anything wrong. In reality I was headed in the direction of my father, with blinders obscuring my perception.

I can recall Timmy, my best friend in high school, telling me Vernon, a bully, threw his books on the floor in first period. Timmy was upset, and I could tell he was holding his tears back while he attempted to tell me the story of what lead Vernon to throw his books in the floor. Timmy's voice was breaking, and the girls in my class were happy to fill in the details. I wasn't certain if the assault on my best friend was a challenge to see if I would defend him and my reputation, or just a display of disrespect for the weak.

Timmy and I were best friends from the fourth grade up until I started my first year of college.

I waited until seventh period, where Timmy, Vernon, and I all attended a rowdy Spanish class together. This was the last class of the day, and most of the students didn't take Spanish seriously, so we used these fifty minutes to socialize and play. Everyone was well aware of the beef from earlier that morning between my best friend and the bully. Students stood outside both doorways of my class. After the late bell rang, teachers and hall monitors instructed students to go to class. I was acting out of character as I sat in my chair quietly, patiently waiting for instructions from my teacher to begin an assignment. The tension was thick, and I could feel everyone's eyes watching not only Timmy's every move but checking for my response to Vernon's threats and jokes that he spat repeatedly all during class.

I tried to convince my best friend to bang Vernon as soon as he took his seat. I assured him if Vernon rose to fight back, I would take over. I explained to Timmy, "I can't get in trouble for fighting anymore, but if you just hit him and we get in trouble, I could always say I was breaking it up."

Timmy never followed through, and eventually Vernon grew tired of making threats and not getting a response. So he took a piece of loose leaf paper, balled it up, and hit Timmy in the back of the head with it.

I turned around and said, "The next time you throw something up here, I'm going to throw these hammers on your ass."

Moments before the bell rang, Vernon threw an empty milk carton in the trash in the opposite direction of Timmy and me. I am sure Vernon assumed because he was a junior and we were freshman's that I would be fearful or respect his seniority. Without a second thought I ran over and began to pound lefts and rights on him until he covered his head and balled up in the fetal position.

I shouted out, "Bitch, I told you don't throw anything else!"

After my teacher pulled me off and cleared the classroom, he wanted to know exactly what was going on between the bully and me. My teacher stood between us as I stared the bully down in a threatening manner. I was afraid of being suspended again, and I came clean. My teacher took pity on me and chose not to send us to the office.

When my teacher stepped in the hallway and asked Timmy what the cause of this outburst was, he replied, "I don't know."

To my surprise months later we received a summons to appear in court. The end result was I walked away with a slap on the wrist and a probation before judgment, all this to defend someone else's honor. Timmy was in court and naturally received a clean break.

It took me until my late twenties to realize that you have to let people handle their own shit and suffer their own consequences.

I've worked since I was fifteen years old. I've had every kind of job you can imagine, and just like in school, I was productive and excelled to management in the most important jobs. I worked at Hechinger's, Target, Wendy's, Toys "R" Us, Lion Brothers Co. Inc., Greek Village Carry Out, BJ's Wholesale Club, I worked for an Architectural firm, also at Rosewood Mental Institution...and the list goes on. My first job was a paper route in my early teens, and then I went on to work with the special education classes in high school.

My family would say to my grandmother Marilyn, "How do you think Tony is going to graduate when he's always home on suspension and then rewarded for his bad behavior?"

Whenever I got suspended, my mom, one of my grandmothers, or even my stepdad, Frog, would come to my school and speak on my behalf. I had a strong, consistent support group. Whenever I was suspended, I would go over to Granny's, watch cable, and chill. I knew I was her baby, and I couldn't do any wrong in her eyes. Plus Granny was mindful that she went through the same thing with my dad. She was sure we were just high spirited and expressed ourselves differently from others at times.

When I was young, I had many aunts and uncles who were addicted to drugs, making most of my cousin's children of addicts. Their moms or dads, or even both in some cases, were addicts. For me, it was both parents but the most significant family member who was an addict was my mom. I was aware that when I was a child my parents both dipped and dabbled in drugs and had fun, because I heard that in the seventies that was the in thing. My mom, Terry, was always proud and radiant; she had a rare beauty that made her powerful with the fewest of words. After I was a teenager, I knew my mom was one who indulged in drugs, but she was so beautiful and innocent it didn't really register like it should have. It was really not obvious to the outsiders looking in either. I remember my cousins and me always saying to one another, "I will never do drugs." Drugs had already hit us so close to home, only a fool would get caught up in the drug game. I later learned to never, say never!

I spent many years trying to hide and cover for my mom. As proud of her as I was, I was ashamed when she would come to the school under the influence, even though she would do a good job of masking the truth. My stepfather sensed this feeling because he paid a lot of attention to me when I was growing up. He would shield me from embarrassment and he helped keep my mom's addiction to a minimum. They were a good unit, and each complimented the other in many areas. Thank GOD for my stepfather. He was an excellent provider, and I was sure he would keep her safe.

The drug game is a dangerous game to play with, especially for a woman with such rare beauty. Knowing my mother had a partner in crime during her addiction calmed my anxieties. Even though my mom was addicted to drugs, she was a very good mom and made me her first priority and struggled hard to overcome her addiction. My mom kept an apartment and maintained a job, so I can assume it's safe to call her a functional addict.

Terry was very attentive and spent a lot of time with me as a child. We were friends, not only mother and child. My mom had me when she was seventeen, and I believe our relative closeness in age is what helped strengthen our relationship. If I had a choice, I wouldn't have had it any other way. My mom was very adamant about me doing my homework as soon as I hit the door from school. When I did my homework, it had to be very neat, or I had to do it over and over until it was up to her standards. After awhile the idea of doing my homework repeatedly didn't bother me much because it built my confidence, proved that I had talent and I started to have a desire to write. I had weekly chores: wash the clothes every other Friday, clean the furniture with Windex and furniture polish, take the trash out daily, clean my room daily, and make my bed the moment my feet hit the floor in the morning. I was rewarded with allowance and I was also threatened that if my chores weren't done properly, I couldn't go over to Granny's (the Honeycomb Hideout). That statement alone would always encourage me to exceed my mom's expectations. Mom started instilling good values at an early age, which helped develop my character and sense of responsibility.

Model

Tony and Courtney

CHAPTER 3

Struggles Of A Man-Child With Mixed Identities

My eleventh grade year, I had my most meaningful relationship. I started dating my first love, Sade. At this point in my life, I had many relationships that never went past second base. I meet Sade in 1995 on the subway parking lot at the carnival in Owings Mills MD. She was absolutely beautiful: Sade had long brown hair, an immaculate body shape, almond-brown eyes, and a smile that would make anyone melt. I was there with my crew, the Sandalwood Spades. We liked to believe we ruled the Owings Mills area.

When I first noticed Sade, I was standing in the parking lot with Eddie, my older cousin on my maternal side of the family. He is cool but he takes pleasure in belittling people, and his plan was to pump me up to approach Sade. His goal was to set me up for failure and get a good laugh at my expense. He and I had a pretty healthy relationship, but I feel like he had some resentment toward me for all the ass whippings his older brother encouraged me to put on him in our youth.

When I spoke to Sade, my game was weak. But she obliged me, and eventually she couldn't stop talking. She told me about her family, her relationship with her parents, her goals, and her ambition. She had my full attention the rest of the night, and I was spending all my money on Sade. Every time someone spoke to me, I replied to them but then focused my attention right back on her. She thought I was cute, and I believe she liked my attentiveness, but I think my popularity is what tipped the scale. I was well respected at the carnival, but that was mainly because we were in the heart of Owings Mills, Maryland, where I lived and attended high school. I ditched my friends and took Sade home, back to Silver Spring, Maryland.

Over the following two months, we would converse every night on the phone until four and sometimes five o'clock in the morning. We enjoyed simple dates and attending parties as a couple. Eventually Sade started to press the sex issue and question why we hadn't had sex yet. The subject began to dominate our conversation, and the opportunity presented itself several times. Considering I was not experienced in that department, I was afraid I wouldn't perform properly and she would leave me.

Sade was so different from the girls I normally dated from around the area or from school. She was the full package: beauty and the brains, with a plan for the future. She wanted to be a dentist and was willing to bear my children.

The first time Sade and I had sex, it at my Cousin Monique's house. Monique and I were Twizzler tight. She was one of the few girls I was comfortable sharing my most intimate secrets with, and I had no shame about fully exposing my true self to her. She was my cousin, but we had a much stronger bond than just first cousins. We were like sister and brother. I didn't mind her being aware of the fact that I was a virgin. My cousin had her own place in the same complex as my mom and I, so I spent a lot of time over at Monique's house, and we had a ball playing house. I was very domestic, and my cousin needed a lot of motivation in that department. Her first child adored me, so our arrangement was comfortable for all parties.

Nique was determined to get me laid and let me see exactly how sexual healing can make everything wrong, feel right. She disclosed her sexual experiences with me in detail and was very graphic. She had a lot of suggestions and input on exactly how I was supposed to perform. In essence, I established my sexual fantasies based on the life and stories that my cousin shared with me.

One night Sade visited me over at my cousin's house. Monique let Sade in and told her I was in the shower. Sade was no stranger to Nique's house. She was not considered a guest, so she was free to move comfortably in our home, with no questions asked. Sade came in the bathroom. At first she didn't speak, and I assumed that it was my cousin entering the bathroom without knocking, because that wasn't unusual if she needed something. To my surprise, Sade was on a mission and wasn't taking no for an answer. She asked me through the shower curtain if she could join me. The question was more like a warning, rather than a request. I was nervous and Sade could tell.

She lit a candle and turned the lights out for my comfort. Sade handled me with perfection, and it was obvious that this wasn't her first encounter with a virgin. She stood in front of me in the shower with her ass pressed against my pelvic area, and she lathered up my wash towel with soap. She bathed herself slowly and never once looked at my private area. After about five minutes, I began to feel my soul pole come to life. As my manhood swelled, my ego grew with every pulse and throb. Once Sade felt me reach my full potential, poking her in her lower back and against her ass, she glanced back at me with a sly smile of contentment. She moved back and forth to the beat and soft sounds of "Slow Wine" by Tony! Toni! Tone' belting from my CD player. The song was programmed on repeat and sat on the base of the toilet tank. She turned to face me and told me she loved me and sealed it with a kiss. She then took my hands from the middle of her back and pulled them down to her ass.

I began to gently caress her ass checks, and she whispered in my ear, "Grab that ass tight. Squeeze dat ass. Boy, that's your ass."

Then she asked me if I wanted her to suck it, and I slowly shook my head no. I couldn't imagine my innocent Sade performing oral sex on any man—not even me.

She moved to the back of the shower with her face against the wall. Sade had one hand on my wrist, and the other hand firmly gripped around my dick. She slowly put the head of my dick in her vagina and moaned, "Yesss, that's it, baby." She whispered as she grinded back and forth, still to the rhythm of the music, "Put it all the way in, baby."

I was comfortable at this point as I softly stroked to the beat of "Slow Wine." I found my own rhythm and paced myself as my strokes increased in speed. I grabbed her waist tight while I approached my climax, moaning and groaning.

Sade replied, "Take it," and at that very moment I released in her.

I laid there on her back for a minute and tried to grasp what just took place.

Sade interrupted my thoughts with her final words of affection, "I love you, boy."

I replied, "I love you too, lil' girl."

Sade stepped out of the shower and quickly got dressed. I reached toward the toilet, grabbed my towel, wrapped it around my waist, and stepped out of the shower.

I peeked out of the bathroom, and Monique was sitting in the dining room, looking at me with a grin that could be the signature smile on the next Kool-Aid package.

I walked in the master bedroom, and Sade followed. Even though my energy was completely drained, I felt like I was sitting on top of the world. I turned my back to Sade as she lay across the full size bed, watching my every move. I could feel her eyes on my back. She told me to turn around, and I ignored her. Thinking to myself: If she sees my piece all shriveled up, it would surely run her ass back to the suburbs with no second thought. I dropped my towel, quickly pulled my boxers up, and put my jeans on. I then turned around to face Sade and jumped on the bed, with my legs hanging off the side of the bed and my chest pressed against Sade's chest. I looked in her eyes and gently kissed her.

I had so many questions running through my mind. Did she enjoy it? Was my piece big enough for her? I even wondered how many partners she really had prior to me. I was worried about if Monique or the kids heard us, but she put my mind at ease because she assured me the radio was up too loud plus it was a quick session. At the time I occupied the master bedroom and my cousin enjoyed staying in the living room because that's where we did most of our entertaining guest and allowed the children to play.

After awhile we walked to Wendy's and got some food for the household. Later that night, my mom dropped the car off to me so I was able to take Sade home. Back in Silver Spring, Sade and I sat in the car on her street about a block away from her home. We conversed about our recent events and decided to go for round two in the car. I had a red Pontiac Firebird with tinted-glass T-tops my mother and Frog gifted me on my 16th birthday. Together Sade and I enjoyed breaking that car in on a regular basis.

A year into our relationship, I transferred to Milford Mill High School, and Sade and I were exploring every sexual avenue known to man. I must admit she completely turned me out. I really didn't enjoy performing oral sex on her and she was fine with that, as long as she could get the wood. Our sex sessions eventually lessened, and that really didn't sit well with Sade. For me change and the distance created a lot of insecurities. Sade blamed that on the fact that I transferred to Milford Mill, but in reality there were a number of reasons we stopped having sex as frequent. The trips were costly, school demanded a lot of my time and energy, and I was working as well. We were in our final years of high school, and I needed to be focused. I believed our relationship was strong enough to deal with the distance between us. Her parents really looked down on me, and they didn't hide the fact that they didn't think highly of me.

Transferring wasn't an option for me. I had been in so many fights at Owings Mills High school the principle threatened to permanently suspend me from Baltimore County public schools. I needed a fresh start, so Granny transferred me to her district school zone, and I moved back with DJ Granny in my junior year.

Shortly after I moved and transferred, I eventually started to lose respect for Sade and wondered if she was having sex sessions with someone else. We stuck together out of respect for the time we invested in our relationship and because the idea of losing someone we thought belonged to just us for so long was not an option.

I noticed her arms were getting thick, and I thought she might be pregnant. Even though we were young, I secretly wanted the rumors to ring true, but Sade assured me she was not with child and she was highly offended when I made reference to her weight. Like most things we discussed, it was a touchy topic. Eventually any little thing created conflict between us, and everything was a problem. Sade and I endured the rest of the school year, and we dated for awhile during the time I attended Catonsville Community College. I was working two jobs, attending college, and trying to be attentive to Sade and keep her happy. I was determined to attend Catonsville, because it was the college my mom went to, but naturally Sade wanted me to attend a college that was convenient for her.

Usually Sade could use control tactics with me and get her way, but my reason for staying at Catonsville was sentimental to me, and I usually don't bend when my mom is involved. It was becoming clear that my relationship with Sade was beginning to be driven by nothing but Svengali-like intentions and expectations. However, I love my mom more than words can begin to express, and she has always been my top priority. It is my greatest desire to live to please GOD then her and hopefully be in a position where I can take care of her. I usually handle my relationships with the same type of respect and dignity as I practice with my mom. However, the two could never compete in the same arena.

After one of our regular fights, Sade played the victim card and admitted to aborting my child. At first I could relate and feel her pain, because it was a forced decision by her father. Sade was very graphic and, I felt at the time, sincere. In the past I had witnessed her father's rage from a far; I saw him slap her, and I was hurt because there was nothing I could do to defend her. When Sade shared the abortion with me for the first time, my first reaction was to just hug her, to let her know everything was all right, so she would be aware that I was on her side.

I had mixed emotions at that time. I felt like I should keep this to myself, because I respected Sade and at the time abortion was a controversial subject that people felt passionate about. I was never in favor of abortions, but I always respected people and their decisions. At this point I witnessed many of my family members and friends overcame this mirrored struggle, so I felt semi-prepared for the overwhelming emotions that come attached after you experience an abortion.

Some of my family members suggested that my girl was pregnant, but I didn't pay it too much attention because the women in my family always had something negative to say about my Sade. I was used to my family being over protective. Sade felt that it was obvious that most people didn't care for her and didn't want us to be together. We were too immature for me to get her to understand my family likes her, but don't like how her family relates to me. She was very smart but too vain to comprehend that to my family I'm just as special as she is to her family. Sade, on the other hand, didn't mind expressing how she didn't care to be around her own family or mine either. Her mom and dad hated the idea that we were friends, and they would give me the look of doom every time they saw Sade and me together. Sade's school prom was the last time I saw her parents, and we had to pretend we were just friends all night. Out of respect for Sade, and so I wouldn't ruin her big night, I suppressed my feelings and acted like it didn't bother me. The only good thing about that night was the pictures turned out good and the attention I received from Sade's friends was validating and comforting.

Tony Toni Tone' and Terry Doll Face
Tee & Tee

CHAPTER 4

Constant Fear

I have always been fearless, and I was always aware that I have a high tolerance for pain. With that being said, I was properly introduced to fear several times over during the late nineties. My mom's addiction was at a pivotal point, and her only eldest living sibling had recently died either of an overdose or a laced hit, but the truth still has yet to be revealed. The death of my uncle affected my mom greatly, and as a result, she relied on what she was familiar with to drown out the pain: the drugs. My stepfather was also losing the self-made battle with his addiction. All of my mom's peer's, friends, and loved ones who accompanied her when she was consumed by her addiction are slowly fading away, lost in institutions and or simply struggling with their own demons.

I would be home, and my friends would knock on my door and say, "Tony, you have to go down to Reisterstown Road. I think your mom is lying in the street."

I would quickly run to her aid and I would be certain not to ridicule or condemn her for her actions because my grandmother, Frog (my stepfather), Frog's mom, and others would show her no mercy, and rightfully so. The family knew my mom was a strong and very determined woman. She was familiar with swimming against the current and making a way for herself and her son. My family would exercise tough love with her. I, on the other hand, would be deeply saddened and hurt, but I remained poised and numb, determined to remain above it all.

We would have family meetings after we encountered events such as this, and people would demand that Terry stop and get herself together. I would remain still while showing no visible pain or concern. At times I had to completely disregard all of the bullshit that surrounded me to survive it.

Otherwise I would be likely to go insane. And there was plenty of nonsense engulfing me every single day to drive me there—into insanity.

My life was in such a whirlwind. I was selling weed in the heart of Owings Mills. I had a connection through my first cousin who resided in Baltimore City, and since I had family in the game, it made it easy for me to do it successfully. She was doing her thing in town, and I quickly followed suit. I knew it wasn't much competition in the county, so I was pleased with the outcome.

I recall when my older cousin Karen, who lived with my grandmother, my mom and I along with her two children, paged me 911. I took a deep breath and thought to myself, "What the hell is going on now?"

Instead of calling, I went straight home. I came in the house and asked my cousin what was wrong. She told me calmly that my mom's friend Joe called and said that Terry was sick and he was bringing her home. The first thought that surfaced in my mind was, "Why didn't she call herself?"

My cousin Karen expected a dramatic response of some sort; however, I just stood there and stared at her blankly without a word. It was as if I was not concerned about the health or well-being of my mother. In reality I was simply pacing my emotions. There had always been events in my life to get overdramatic about. Overreactions only served to push me closer to the edge of insanity. One can never control the amount of stimuli in their lives, but I could control my response to them. So I remained calm and logical, again using a brief meditation technique of emotional withdrawal.

My cousin became confused by my lack of response and asked me, "What's going on with you guys?" She argued, "If something is wrong with Terry, we are going to fuck Joe up."

I responded with a simple question: "Why are you whispering?"

She looked at me and was even more confused. She couldn't seem to figure me out. She was used to me responding in a defensive or violent manner. Protecting home, to me, was like breathing air; it was a natural impulse. My cousin Karen and I was always close, she loved me like a son, but also treated me with the level of respect one would exhibit with a close friend. I would imagine because my grandmother helped raise her like a sister to my mom, I related more to her as a good friend or a cool aunt.

She reached out to hold my hand across the table and said to me, "What are you thinking about right now?"

I faced her, slid my hand away, and replied, "Why?"

Karen was at a complete loss for words.

Seconds later Karen's son ran in the house screaming, "Terry and Joe just pulled up!"

When Karen and I approached the car, my mom was completely unconscious but still breathing. I carried my mom into the house while my cousin dialed 911. I couldn't begin to express the cold, empty feeling that penetrated through my veins as I internalized the events taking place at that moment.

When the paramedics arrived at my home, they quickly began to work on my mom. After a while she had been ruled out, considered dead, and they tried every avenue to resuscitate her. My home was full of strangers, and they were working diligently to save my mom as my family and I shadowed them, watching their every move. The lead paramedic holding my mom's life in his hands was a high school classmate who graduated a few years before me unfortunately I had beaten him up several years ago.

I was so afraid. I closed my eyes and began to silently pray as tears rolled down my checks. I begged and pleaded with GOD. I had so many mixed emotions, but the fear surpassed all of my feelings by far. I was left with only one choice: hold on to my faith and wait on my GOD.

Anthony

Tony

CHAPTER 5

Who's In Control?

At age twenty-one, my dad was still locked up and had been in prison since I was a small child. My only consistent male role model was my stepfather, Frog. Not only was he my stepdad, but he is a true friend. My stepfather, Frog, had been with us since I was ten years old. He was my mom's other half and now he was arrested as well. This in turn forced me to worry and look after my mom even more than before. I was in the habit of masking my problems and dealing with the blows as they came.

Around that time Sammy, my cousin on my maternal side of the family, began to visit me more frequently. I always enjoy his company but his visits always came with a price or a side bar coupled with a new strange group of hungry hovering friends. He would come over to my house, cop a bag of weed, pay half price, or borrow some money and tell me he was headed to Washington DC. In the past he had always been shy and timid; I had fought all his battles and was his spokesman for many years. Recently he had been more outgoing and outspoken. I really approved of this sudden change and was happy for him. For some odd reason, Sammy was adamant about me accompanying him to DC. I would always agree to join him, but I would never follow through.

Finally I chose to oblige him and go to DC. I was aware that he was reaching out to me, and I was confident this forty-five minute trip would reveal the truth about Sammy and his struggles. Of course the trip answered the questions that where highlighted in my mind. Twenty minutes into the ride, after talking in circles and making me promise not to judge or disown him, he finally came out to me as being gay.

When we reached our destination, a popular club called Tracks, I was amazed. I had never seen, in one place, at one time, so many different types of homosexuals and people who lead alternative lifestyles being completely comfortable with their authentic selves. I was shocked and amazed, but I remained at bay and I was quiet the whole night.

Sammy tried to encourage me to loosen up and dance; I chose not to. I felt everyone staring and admiring my good looks. People were very attentive yet cautious about approaching me. I felt like a celebrity. I liked the fact that people where offering me drinks and inviting me to other clubs. I sensed that I intimidated most people in the gay clubs, not in an aggressive manner but in more of a sexual or competitive fashion.

It was over a month before I returned to Club Tracks. I needed awhile to digest this new scene. When I arrived at Tracks for the second time, I was fully prepared and confident. I saw Dwayne, a gentleman I met the first time I visited. Dwayne was delighted to see me and embraced me with a hug, like I was the highlight of his evening.

We spoke briefly before he was compelled to remind me that he had warned me before that I would return and he would be waiting. That subject was one of the select few we hadn't seen eye to eye on when I was there last. Most people would have been modest in that area, however Dwayne didn't hesitate to remind me that he knew I would return. I stressed to him once again that I was straight and I was just supporting my cousin and his decision to live a life that not everyone in our family or immediate circle totally agreed with. This time he and I talked all night, until 6:00 a.m. when the club closed.

We exchanged numbers, and we started to develop an innocent relationship. He began to come to visit me in Baltimore on the Marc Train. Dwayne started to take me out to dinner or to the movies, and we frequently visited the Inner Harbor, comedy shows, and poetry events. He never once approached me in an inappropriate manner or made any passes toward me. But it was evident that in the event that I was ready to explore new horizons, he wanted to be the first to introduce me to bigger and better things.

I finally decided to visit Dwayne in DC on my own. I had become comfortable in his company and developed a new found trust for the friendship we built. My only challenge was sharing a twin bed with him that was located on the third floor, because we all know what happens when (the heat starts to rise—go figure). I would always sleep in my sweatpants and a T-shirt. He in turn would sleep in his boxers or his briefs. This was the first time I had ever experienced a relationship where I was constantly validated, complimented and treated with genuine respect.

I was impressed because he always greeted me with small gifts and paid when we went out. Our dates gradually evolved into shopping sprees at his expense, and he was far from frugal, I might add. I could finally really escape reality. I was completely stress-free in DC.

After about a month or two, I was anxious to try male-on-male sex, but I didn't want the title "Gay" or "Homosexual," so I put off having sex, which I knew was soon to take place.

I finally rationalized and reasoned with myself, "If I penetrate *him*, I'm not *gay*. Besides, no one else will ever know, because I'm here in DC."

One day Dwayne and I, along with several of his friends, visited Georgetown to do lunch at a local gay book store that sold books, coffee and food. From there we went shopping and we capped the night off with a couple drinks and a few hands of spades over one of his friend's house. After an eventful day, we decided to venture back home while we have the benefit of the cool night air. We were feeling no pain at his place, due to the fact that we were both drunk.

I waited for a while after we had each showered, and then I got comfortable in bed and removed my sweatpants. The simple gesture was his invitation, and before my sweatpants hit the floor, Dwayne made his move. He was on top of me, kissing me passionately while slowly grinding his private parts against mine. After grinding for a few minutes, we were fully erect. Dwayne began to caress my waist then started to make love to my whole body with just his tongue and his hands alone. Dwayne was licking my toes while caressing my man tool when he realized, I was about to reach my climax. He quickly yet gently slid his muscular body on top of me, and once again we were chest to chest and dick to dick. With both of our dicks in one of his hands, I exploded. Once our encounter was finished, I felt satisfied but puzzled and ashamed. I enjoyed this experience, and up until this point I had always wondered what he meant when he would say, "Sex is not all about penetration."

Over the next few days, I pondered about how this event pleased me and, more importantly, how it pleased Dwayne. I felt as though Dwayne had won the challenge and taken complete control of our sex session. That thought alone didn't sit well with me. Sex to me could only go one of two ways: either I was going to turn you completely out, or I was going to be turned out. Sex was not supposed to be just all right; it's either good or bad. And although I took sex as a challenge, I felt it was always supposed to be pleasurable for both parties.

On the third night after we had our first encounter, I had mastered the game in my mind and was ready to practice. When Dwayne came home from work that evening, we had dinner. I prepared baked chicken, baked macaroni and cheese, canned collard greens, and oven-baked biscuits. After dinner we took a shower together for the first time and then sat out on the roof, which was actually an unfinished semi-private patio area. This was the most peaceful and calm setting. The sky was pitch-black, and the stars were bright white, which made the sky appear dark blue. There we smoked a blunt and consumed a few drinks of Hennessy and Coke. Unaware I was embracing this newfound lifestyle; I was getting to know a new side of me.

For the first time, I was comfortable walking around in my Ralph Lauren quarter-length robe and black Calvin Klein boxer briefs that he purchased from Hecht's.

He commented, "I was beginning to think you didn't like the underwear and tank tops I brought you. I thought I would never see you in them."

I replied, "Don't wreck your brain worrying about getting me in my briefs. Focus on getting me out of my underwear, that's where the real challenge sets in."

When we went back in the house, I decided to make my move. I put my private parts right in Dwayne's face while he sat on the floor with his back against the bed, sorting CDs and nursing his last glass of Hennessy and Coke. He smiled and was overjoyed with this newfound confident and aggressive Tony. Dwayne began to massage my testicles and bite and nibble on the base of my manhood through my boxer briefs. I pulled my briefs down to my thighs, grabbed the crown of his head with my left hand, and grabbed the base of my dick with my right hand.

I whispered to him, "Are you hungry, baby?"

He replied, "Um hum."

I repeatedly smacked my strong, thick, fully erect, two-toned caramel and black dick against his cheeks and lips. In between the smacks, I would occasionally stick my power tool all the way in the back of his throat, so far Dwayne would almost gag, but he would always manage to control his reflex. It was evident he couldn't take the whole piece of wood in his mouth, but that didn't stop me from attempting to achieve the impossible. I gathered that was a major turn-on for Dwayne.

I motioned to him to stand up. As soon as his feet hit the floor and we were eye level, I gently pushed Dwayne backward onto the bed and, in a low but firm tone, I told him to lie down. I stepped completely out of my boxers and began to show Dwayne how to really grind a nigga out. I was determined to leave a lasting and a memorable impression on him.

After I was certain he was stimulated to the fullest extent, I said, "Turn dat ass over, boy, and give me some of that boy pussy."

Dwayne rolled on his stomach and requested that I be easy with him.

I replied, "I'm a-break you in easy, boy."

I grabbed out of the top nightstand drawer a condom along with a bottle of baby oil. I greased his ass up thoroughly and massaged oil onto his shoulder blades, up and down his neck, down his spine, and, of course, the spot that received the most attention: his lower back. While massaging Dee's back, I was grinding my dick up and down the crack of his ass and the back of his legs.

When I finally stuck the head in Dwayne, he screamed out, "Awwh, please be easy!"

I penetrated Dwayne slowly while I bit the back of his neck and gripped his mid-back firmly. I whispered, "Relax, baby and let me get it all the way in. Once it's open, it won't hurt so much. Just relax."

After I got it all the way in, I felt Dwayne's muscles relax, and I shifted gears. His every wall was stamped with my big brown dick, with that thick black ring around the head. I banged his walls out to the left for a while: bang, bang, bang. Then to the right: bang, bang. Then once again to the left: bang, bang, bang. After I would tease the walls with painful pleasure, I would drop that dick down low. Then I would jump right back in rhythm while Janet Jackson's soft words of "Any Time, Any Place" played loudly on the surround sound.

After Dwayne released himself all over the sheets, I pulled myself out, removed the condom, and busted off all over his back. From the look on Dwayne's face, it was a job well done. I was satisfied and exhausted, and then he wanted to talk, so I obliged him.

He asked me, "Are you sure this is your first gay relationship?"

I answered him with a simple yes and sealed it with a slight smile. As I stared aimlessly at the ceiling, he laid in my right arm, and I could feel his eyes looking up at me. He began to compliment me on how good my love-making was and how pretty my dick was. Dwayne explained that it wasn't just the good lovin' that separated me from your average dude; it was the longevity that had him blown away. He explained most men with good wood were two-minute brothers and showed no signs of affection after sex. He told me I was good at what I did and that I seemed to be cut from a different cloth.

After about seven months, I began to catch Dwayne in pointless lies, and I took that as the ultimate form of disrespect. I've always believed a liar is a thief, and I would rather disassociate myself from someone instead of waiting for an ugly ending. I've never liked confusion in my relationships. Trust and communication are top priority in any relationship I put my time, energy, and, more importantly, my feelings into.

I decided to draw him in a little more and be certain he was absolutely head over heels for me. Then my next move was to totally remove myself abruptly from Dwayne and the relationship. My primary goal was to break his heart and show him how it feels when you put your trust into someone and then have your trust betrayed. Ideally I wish I could have ended the relationship and continue to build a solid friendship, but that was impossible to do with him and his emotions. My unexpected withdrawal from Dwayne devastated and broke his heart.

After the breakup it was years later when Dwayne his friends and I attended a special gospel services in Laurel Maryland. The evening ended at a popular bar and lounge in DC. It was evident he still had an emotional connection and he wanted to pick up where we left off. For me sex was not an option and a relationship was not even up for discussion, so I chose to make that our last visit.

When we initially broke up I felt empowered and amused with his attempts to reconstruct a relationship that was fictitious. At times I considered ending the fantasy on a positive note, but it was easier to be realistic and direct. I wanted to let him see that young is not always a replica of dumb, and some people are not willing to settle for just anything. Even if that came with the price of our friendship, my mind was made up; because if its starts with lies, I'm certain it will end in the same fashion. That became a regular routine for me: I would love 'em, leave 'em, and keep them wanting more. It was my defense mechanism.

Back at home in Baltimore, my mom, Terry, was overcoming her addiction and diligently striving to strengthen her relationship with Jehovah to become a baptized witness. My stepdad, Frog, was still incarcerated and striving to achieve the same goals. My mom and I would visit my stepdad twice a month down on Eastern Shore. At the time I had a strong desire to confide my sexual truth to my stepdad, but after thinking it through further, I chose not to. I was afraid of disappointing my stepdad, but more importantly I was afraid of breaking my mom's heart, so sharing my sexuality was a subject that was not up for discussion. I felt that Terry and Frog were finally on one accord again, and they were determined to take control of their own lives. As eager as I was to share the recent events with someone I loved and I was certain loved me, I chose not to. I allowed denial to overwhelm my mind. I just believed that as long as I never was penetrated, I was not a gay man. I thought to myself this was just a onetime occurrence or a phase that would soon pass.

Terry and Frog were planning on getting married, and I was pleased with this idea; Frog had been a part of my life since I was in the fourth grade, and I would be pleased to give him my mom's hand in marriage. My mom is my best friend, and I admired her for her strength and endurance. She was a solider determined to land on her feet and weather any storm. No matter what adversity she faced, she persevered and came out with a smile. That was a quality I was determined to emulate.

It wasn't long before my stepdad was released, and at this time Terry was baptized and a pioneer in her congregation. Frog was in the process of being baptized and preaching the word also. He and I started a weekly one-on-one Bible study, and naturally the meetings felt good and were effective, but I was consumed by the world and faced with many new challenges at that time in my life. It was apparent at that present time I appreciated the bible studies, but looking back I feel I wanted and needed some fatherly support. Eventually the Bible studies became more and more inconsistent, and I had to tell my stepfather I wanted to temporarily stop and I could possibly start again in the near future.

A few years later, he announced he was getting married to another woman, and I was disappointed and angry. Once again I felt betrayed and abandoned. I was upset because I never imagined Frog would be the cause of so much pain in my mom's life. It was a ritual I had grown accustomed to: trust any man and he will break your heart. Frog continued to visit and remain cordial with my grandmother, my mom, and myself. Terry was poised and remained focus on serving her GOD. One year after Frog was married, he began to converse with Terry, and we were confused whether he was seeking a relationship or if he just needed forgiveness to ease his conscience. If his reputation was the dividing factor to determine his intent, it would prove he had good objective and was operation from a sincere and Christ like place. Still my adolescence surpassed my maturity level when addressing matters of the heart and I felt the way he handled the situation was wrong, but Terry was at peace with it. She explained that there was no reason to be angry, because everything happens for a reason. She said "he will always be a part of us, but GOD had another path for her to follow". After some time I found peace with the situation when I realized everyone has challenges and adversities, and until I walk a mile in someone's shoes, I shouldn't judge (**Matthew** 7: 1-5) [Refer to chapter 11]

Tony and Mark going to Martins West for a
New Year's Eve Party

CHAPTER 6

The In-Between Time

I took a few months to focus on myself. I just wanted to work and try to enjoy life. I was working at K-mart, and every night I would come home from work and for some reason Sherri would be over at Granny's house, sitting on the sofa, blushing at me. At the time my cousin Warren and I were both staying at Granny's house. His girlfriend had a cousin, Sherri, who would visit with her every day. Eventually we started kicking it. Sherri wanted to know why I was so serious and reserved. She wanted me to let her in my world or my head, or better yet, in my pants. Sherri grew on me fast, and I enjoyed her company in a platonic way, and her kids were cool as a fan. When we all went out or to church, her two sons would parade me around and always introduce me as their dad. That felt good, but it also made me proceed with caution, but it didn't stop the desire to get a taste of Sherri's pie.

She kept me intrigued and in good spirits, considering it had been a while since the last time I had sex. The more time I spent with Sherri, the more I craved her. I was struggling with the idea of sharing with Sherri my past endeavors, but I knew it was mandatory to tell her before we took the next step to intimacy. Eventually things started to heat up with Sherri and me, so I decided to tell Sherri that I slept with a man in the past. That plan simplified this complicated situation and in-turn allowed Sherri to have a choice and that forced the ball in her court. When I shared my secret, I kept it real simple and I was certain not to give any details.

Her response shocked me. She told me she knew I messed around, and she was in the life as well. I was appalled and embarrassed. She told me it was cool and I was just her type: clean-cut, neat, soft-spoken, and a little on the feminine side.

I responded with a sarcastic, "Thanks. I don't know if that was an insult or a compliment." We laughed and Joked and formed a sudden closeness, which later evolved into a lifelong friendship. It felt good to relieve myself of the boulders I was carrying on my shoulders. I knew at that point I was going to get a taste of Sherri.

Sequentially we decided to make the following night our debut, at my house. I set the mood with some vanilla velvet candles and some smooth grove music, coupled with a set of new curtains and a matching comforter set for my bed. When Sherri arrived, I was lying in the middle of the bed with my hand in my boxers, playing with my Johnson.

She smiled and said, "This is my shit. Get up and dance for me, baby."

I was shocked, and that request totally threw my whole game for a loop. I said, "Naw, I only dance in the club, baby girl."

She replied, "You just scared."

She was grinding and pumping her pelvis while she slowly undressed. I watched her every move in awe. She was now naked down to her Victoria's Secret panties; her breasts were small with big, black, perky nipples.

She said, "Come on, baby."

Then she grabbed my hand and stood me up and pressed her pelvic area against my ass and wined with me. She guided me and talked me through each motion step by step as she instructed me to put my back into it and dance like I was fucking. Sherri told me to close my eyes and imagine I was alone.

I remember her saying, "Just feel the music, and don't be afraid to touch yourself."

I began to relax and loosen up.

Sherri softly said, "Always seduce your audience. You have the power to make anyone want you, because you are beautiful, but you have to embrace that and keep it highlighted in your mind at all times."

We both smiled and we began on our journey to explore one another, making the night one that I will never forget. She taught me the art of seduction and gave me a lesson on lovemaking.

I was floored, because I always thought that I was the best that ever did it on the dance floor, on the court, in the bedroom, and anywhere else for that matter.

Sherri pressed repeat and set track number five on the CD player, "Mary Go Round," belted out of the speakers on Musiq Soul child's first album, *Aijuswanaseing*. Sherri told me once again to close my eyes, feel the music, and touch myself, and I complied. When I opened my eyes, she was lying on the bed, with the lights on low. Her legs were wide open while she played with her pussy. The roles had reversed on me with the blink of my eye. I laid on top of her and kissed her ever so gently while I slowly caressed her outer thighs and massaged her waist. I slid down with my rock hard dick pressed against her inner thigh. I put one of her big black nipples in my mouth so I could suck it while caressing the other. Finally I stuck my middle finger inside her, and then I put my other two fingers inside Sherri. It was so soft, wet, and warm, so I assumed she came. It wasn't until we slept together several times that I knew her pussy was just naturally that good and wet.

Just when I was reaching for a condom to strap up and tap that ass, she rolled me over and performed oral sex on me, and it was the best head I ever had. At this point three other people perform oral sex on me, and she was the first to get the whole dick in her mouth. It felt like a gentle massage, the feeling was surreal to me. I just laid back and closed my eyes and moaned into ecstasy. She sucked it gently for awhile and nibbled on the head, then she sucked real hard as she went all the way down on my Johnson. Then she would come all the way up with her jaws locked tight. It was a painful pleasure. Then she would go all the way back down on my meat and graze her teeth against the base of my dick. Finally I stood up, and she bent over the bed. I began to penetrate her gently with just the head and half of the wood.

She moaned with pleasure. "Yeah, baby. That's it, baby. You hittin' my spot, baby."

I pulled out because I felt myself reaching my climax. I then laid across the bed, and Sherri climbed on top of me and rode my dick like a rodeo cowgirl. She swirled and twirled that ass while she popped that pussy.

She asked, "Whose dick is this, huh, nigga?"

I grabbed her around the waist and tried to take control, slamming her all the way down on my dick. She began to scream out in pain, and her legs began to shake.

I told her, "Buss off on that dick, bitch," as I continued to pound that pussy out.

Finally I pulled out and laid back on the bed with my feet on the floor. Sherri dropped to her knees between my legs, and then I came all over her breast.

Sherri and I kicked it for about four months. When we went out, I would discreetly check out the guys, and Sherri, on the other hand, would clearly check for the girls. Sherri liked to pop E-pills at the time, and she would get a little loose. I in turn would have to spend half the night babysitting her. The more time we spent together, the more comfortable I became with the idea of dating a man. Sherri and I maintained a genuine and lifelong friendship.

After awhile I started dating Gerald. He was a very serious and cocky man, and his pockets ran deep, which gave him presidency over our relationship. Every weekend Gerald suggested we go to Atlantic City and stay at the Trump Plaza. Over time I learned he was an extremist, and one who was quick to claim you as his trophy w,, ho loved to gamble and spend his money. After dating him for only a few months, I mastered the game twenty-one, also called blackjack, and adopted a newfound addiction. He was in the closet and treated me very well, but he was accustomed to getting what he wants so it wasn't a surprise when I fell for him. I realized he was intrigued by me and claimed me as his new accessory. I imagined he thought because he was introducing me to new places and things I was caught up and lost my head about him. Even though Gerald was the first man I ever allowed to penetrate me he still had yet to witness my alter ego and see just how strong willed I really was. We would have around-the-worlds on a regular basis; he'd fuck me, and I in turn would fuck him. The sex was all right, yet still I honestly fell for this dude. Our relationship lasted for about a year and six months. Gerald had two children, two jobs, a baby mother at home, and me. Everything was in doubles with this dude but it didn't offend me much because at this point I was still studying him and learning his routine so I could determine his authentic intent.

One day we were shopping in Reisterstown Plaza a semi ghetto shopping mall located on the cross lines of Baltimore City and Baltimore County, when we ran into Gerald's ex-lover, Chris. To my surprise he got out of pocket with me. I took that as a proposal to fight, so I kindly obliged him and invited Chris to the parking lot to discuss matters further. Gerald's car was parked out in front of the main lobby. He told me to be cool and act my age. I didn't reply and continued to walk in the direction of his brand new white Altima with dark illegal tints and fresh chrome rims. I was certain Gerald was afraid his ex-lover was going to hurt me, and that made me even more anxious to run a demo on this cat.

Gerald kept telling me to get in the car, because it wasn't worth it. He warned me, "That nigga is going to come with all those boys, and you are too cute to be fighting in the parking lot at this ghetto-ass mall."

I had my mind made up and was determined to bring this disrespect to an end before it snowballed into something even worse. The last time Chris and Gerald spoke; Gerald told me Chris said, "he was going to fuck my lil' ass up on first sight". I replayed his threats in my mind over and over again as I leaned against the trunk of Gerald's car with one foot on the rear bumper and the other foot planted securely on the ground.

I spotted Chris with his entourage across the parking lot coming in my direction. He was running his mouth with his finger in the air and a corona beer bottle in his other hand. I just waited until he got within arm's length, and I pushed off of Gerald's car with my left foot and punched Chris in his noise with my right fist. His face split wide open on the first blow. He fell back, put his head down, and charged me. I dropped my left guard down and uppercut him once again with my famous left.

Meanwhile his friends screamed out to Chris, "You better fuck his little ass up, beat the shit out of him." That of course fueled me even more and took me from hundred to a hundred and ninety-nine in two seconds flat.

My friend Gerald just stood still in awe.

When Chris hit the ground, I jumped on him, pinned him down with my knees on both his forearms, and began to pound down rights and lefts.

Finally Gerald defused the situation and brought me back to reality by calling out to me, "Tony, Tony, chill. You got work done, kid." As he put his hands on my shoulders, he said, "Let's go before five-o [the police] come."

When I stood up, my new Maurice Malone jeans and button-down shirt was covered in blood. As I went to get in Gerald's car, Chris struggled to his feet and charged me while I had one foot in the car and one planted on the ground. I heard his footsteps and turned around and kicked him in his face. When the kick connected, his body fell like dead weight, and his keys flew out of his pocket. I calmly walked over, picked his keys up, and asked his friends if anyone would like to be next, but they stood speechless.

Gerald was still in awe and praised me all the way home. He told me my little ass could really fight.

I asked him, "Did you think that it was going to go any other way?"

He replied, "Honestly, I thought I was going to have to fuck dem' niggas up for you, 'cause Chris is a big nigga like me and you see he is cut the fuck up, plus he be running them niggas around Park Heights."

I said, "Yeah, he is running *through* them faggots, but he's not running any real niggas up the Heights." Then I threw his keys out the window on the highway as Gerald proceeded to drive me home back to the county.

When my relationship ended with Gerald, I met some new friends. For a little over a year or so, we'd spend time hanging in the clubs and partying outside of the club scene. As a group we were always the showstopper, the center of attention: dancing against people, getting into fights, and just having fun. We decided to call ourselves the Super Friends, only among ourselves. No one could pick their own name; it had to fit your character and be of the opposite sex. The Super Friends were Maurice/Wonder Woman (she turns it), may he rest in peace; Lou/Aqua Woman (Real Fish), may he rest in peace; Nard/Rainbow Bright (she's colorful & smiles); Taavon/Poison Ivy (she's fierce); Marty/Cat Woman (sneaky); Mike/Red Sonya (high yellow); Jay/ Xena Warrior Princess (she's a big girl); Manny/Isis (sexy glossy eyes/she's slick); Steven/Fire Starter (the shit starter); and of course me, Tony/Queen Cleopatra.

Many of my friends at the time were extremely active sexually. I was trying to practice abstinence. Occasionally Gerald, my ex, would call to take me away for the weekend. Usually I would fall short in my attempts to remain celibate when it came to Gerald, but aside from him I was disciplined and respected my standards.

Eventually I met Mark in a popular club called Sportsman's, located in downtown Baltimore. He was an older distinguished gentleman. I was attracted to him because he was soft-spoken but yet very social. Although I found him attractive and enjoyed his conversation, I didn't see a future with him, nor could I imagine having a lasting relationship with him. Mark was tall, with a bald head, walnut-brown eyes, goatee, and a smile that would demand any crowd's attention. I didn't like the idea that Mark worked at Sportsman's bar located in downtown Baltimore off and on and hosted karaoke. He was there on days he worked and days he didn't work. Honestly, he was there every day. Eventually I started to visit the bar just to hang with Mark and talk shit while we shot the breeze until the bar closed. Mark and I would close the bar, turn the slow jams on, and play cards with a select few friends.

It was only a short while before we broke the cycle and found ourselves with no chaperone, alone in the bar. We conversed about our mutual attraction and what route our friendship would take if we pursued a more intimate relationship. Mark and I kissed passionately for the first time, and he caressed my back and ran his fingers through my hair. I was turned on and decided to take Mark home with me to Granny's house, where I was residing at the time.

When we got to the house, we looked at some pictures in my photo album while we sat up and talked all morning. Then we cuddled, and I slept like a baby.

After we spent a few weekends together, I was compelled to test the waters. I was intrigued by Mark's patience and respect. Our weekends where made even more special when my grandmother, Mark and I created a routine that entailed coffee and breakfast in the morning, couple with lunch and a Madea play. That would evolve to dinner over laughs, and live entertainment as Mark would religiously sing to granny. Time would always get away from us as the company was highly preferred from all spectrums we resembled the modern day Golden girls with a tan as we sat, ate, conversed and commented on everything and everyone. The way Mark was able to understand and relate to me and grannies relationship floored me and made me even more attracted to him. I was certain if I didn't make a move soon, we would remain bunk buddies, and my curiosity would never be satisfied. The following weekend Mark stayed over at my house. I took a shower early and conveniently left my towel on my bed where Mark waited patiently. After I lathered up thoroughly, I screamed out to Mark to bring me a towel. He responded seconds later with a slight tap on the bathroom door.

Mark waited for me to reply, and I said, "It's open."

He opened the door slowly. I never looked up, and I never made eye contact. I could feel Mark's eyes on me, so I stepped into the water to wash the soap suds off while moving in a slow circle. Stroking my manhood with one hand and caressing my ass with the other, I occasionally rubbed my chest in a downward and seductive motion to assist the water in washing the soap suds off. I then reached down to turn the water off, and opened the sliding glass shower door. Then I stepped out of the shower. I looked Mark in his eyes and thanked him as I grabbed the towel and thoroughly dried off. Mark went back in my bedroom and waited for me to return.

I applied tea tree oil from head to toe and dressed in a white tank top, some black Express boxer briefs, and my red hooping basketball shorts, which hung low. At this point I had Mark exactly where I wanted him: wanting more. Every piece of me flirted with the idea of sharing myself with him, but I was certain I needed to exercise patience and remain discipline.

I had to deny myself once again, if I wanted to be in control and nourish this relationship and make it blossom into something real. In my mind I was convinced we were from two different worlds, but I saw so much potential in Mark. He had many qualities I was drawn to. Even though my gut said no, my heart was longing for a friend, a companion, someone to build a future with and someone to fulfill my passionate appetite. It was imperative that I be still and deny the flesh. It was a crucial period for Mark and me. I wanted to keep him intrigued without being intimate but yet remain seductive. Although I wanted more than anything to get a taste of that vanilla swirl, it was more important to build our trust and friendship outside of the gay society and among the heterosexual world and, more importantly, among our families. To my surprise Mark was very family oriented and was pretty even-keeled when it came to the straight society: a major plus in my book. With all these good qualities, I was certain the sex would be whack.

We were both patient, and the opportunity presented itself several times. I realized I wasn't teasing him anymore, nor was I just keeping him intrigued. I was scared and this had a reverse effect on my game.

When the time came to turn Mark out, I was frozen still. I was in a trance and didn't know what direction to go in next. All of my skill and technique went away. That didn't stop Mark from making his move though. Mark gently, but yet with a masculine touch, massaged my body all over. In addition to the traditional massage he allowed his tongue worked magic and blew my mind. I was amazed and caught off guard. After I reached my climax, just by Mark's majestic touch and tongue, he climbed on top of me, sat on my lap, and busted off all on my stomach and chest.

I thought to myself, "This is the second time I've experienced Niagara Falls, live in the flesh."

Mark took his T-shirt off and wiped my stomach and chest dry. He laid on my chest, and I felt mixed emotions starting to surface. I felt full satisfaction coupled with shame and embarrassment. We had a deep conversation as we lay naked and cuddled. We expressed how we felt, what we liked and didn't like. I shared with Mark that I didn't perform oral sex, and he expressed how he didn't get penetrated. This last statement raised a red flag.

I thought to myself, "He doesn't get penetrated—imagine that. But of course he expected to taste my lemon meringue pie, my crème de la crème."

I saw that as a challenge and an opportunity to put his words to the test and redeem myself.

Mark told me he loved me many times before, but I felt if he wanted to express his love for me, he would allow me to penetrate him. I never hesitated to stress the issue. In addition to this newly found challenge, I promised myself never to allow anyone to penetrate me without being able to return the favor, and I never break my promises. So we were caught between a rock and a hard place, a catch-22 situation. But, once again, Mark shocked the hell out of me when he agreed to allow me to penetrate him but at another time, and I agreed.

Our dating scene was awesome. He always welcomed my mentally challenged Aunt and the children in our families with pleasure, to accompany us when we went out. We went to the movies, bowling, to the Inner Harbor, Go cart racing, amusement parks, trips out town and, of course, to the clubs as a unit, promoting our newly formed relationship. The Lovemaking was occasional but still passionate yet tasteful encounters. Our intimacy consisted more of lovemaking, grinding, and becoming familiar with our likes and dislikes, hot spots and not spots.

Finally I performed fellatio on Mark with the intention of getting some boy pussy, and he kindly returned the favor. When I released myself, Mark was sure I was done for the evening. When I whispered in his ear that I wanted some booty, he was shocked and disappointed, but he honored his word and he agreed.

I began to grind my wood on his lower back and on his ass. I could tell when I put the head in that he wasn't used to getting wood on a regular basis. Mark wasn't shy with his moans of discomfort and pain. I wanted to stop because he fulfilled his promise, but it was good and I had been holding back for so long it was hard for me to pull out. It was obvious the pleasure was one-sided. I was really confused now. I was angry for having to stop, but yet still I was drawn to Mark. That created closeness with him but also an anger toward him.

After we laid in complete silence for a while, Mark regrouped and returned the favor. He expressed his anger through his sex, and surprisingly I loved it. With the entire lovemaking sessions, I didn't think the natural romantic had an animal instinct, but he fooled my ass. I felt like a human rag doll. My legs were bent back as he long stroked and banged my walls out. Just when Mark could sense I couldn't take any more, he flipped me over and hit it doggy-style. I moaned and groaned in painful bliss—more pain than bliss. Once again I felt those mixed emotions. I was pleased but disappointed that he got his man and I didn't. I figured our relationship would be short-lived because I'm versatile and he was not.

Our relationship lasted about eight months. We had developed a solid friendship with one another's families, which made breaking up even more difficult than I had imagined. I had made my mind up and I decided that it was time for our relationship to come to an end. It was a challenging process because I knew it would be painful for me and more so for Mark. It was even more intense because I felt like I was breaking up with not only Mark but with his whole family. I really cared for many of his family members. However, I cut all ties with Mark, aside from being cordial or simply saying hi in passing.

Carla and Cori, his nieces, and I remained friends through it all. Carla and I spent a considerable amount of time together. Cori has always been an excellent confidant, someone who is always in support of my goals and dreams. I'm sure we bonded so well because she has a great deal of drive and ambition but she is never too cocky to take advice. They were both as fine as they wanted to be. The more time Carla and I spent together the more I enjoyed her company. We had similar outlooks on life, and we both enjoyed smoking weed occasionally, having deep conversations, having spade parties, and we even visited my church Scripturally Sound together. Carla encouraged Mark and I to be a couple again because she had a lot of faith in us being a positive pair. Even still, she never harassed me when I was out and when I demanded the attention of our surroundings; she supported my decision to be a single man and respected my wishes. Carla was always a lady, but she knew exactly when to unleash that thug. I loved her company because together we were a force to be reckoned with. I was confident she would defend my honor in any situation, whether I was present or not, that confirmed and made me certain the love we shared was genuine and our friendship was free of biasness.

At the time I had attachment as well as trust issues, and I dealt with everyone outside my family with a long-handled spoon: my friends, my lovers, and at times some of my family members. I was unaware of these issues, so I was a friend to many, because people were always drawn to me, but I would never consider people my friends. I was sure they would only disappoint me in due time. If I was hungry, I wouldn't even consider asking friends for money, even if I was sure they would be honored to give or lend it me. I would rather have had a stranger buy me a drink before I would even consider allowing a so-called friend treat me. And yet, for some odd reason, I felt connected with both Carla and Cori. Cori was a workaholic and determined to be a success and she has always been wise beyond her years. I felt they were a lot like me in many ways. Carla was good as gold, as real as they come, and sharp as a whip. However, she didn't take any shit, and she was never shy about expressing herself, be it verbally or physically.

Tony Rone Chico'

CHAPTER 7

A Long Dance With The World's Strongest Boy: "Heroin"

When I returned to the gay scene as a single man, I began to hang out with the Super Friends once again. I was about twenty three back in the clubs, having house parties, enjoying the single life, and chilling with my friends. We kicked it for about six months, and many hidden attractions were revealed. I was well aware that almost all the Super Friends dates and lovers were interested in or at least attracted to me. What came to me as a surprise was the fact that my homeboys themselves saw me in that fashion. My friends were never bothered by their dates' interest in me, because they were familiar with the games this lifestyle played. Aside from that, they all knew it wasn't in my character to even entertain that idea of hooking up with their dates.

At this juncture all my friends had expressed or showed some signs of interest in me. These invites were usually expressed in a subtle or sarcastic way in our games of truth or dare. I made it clear off the top: "It ain't happening." I loved them in a brotherly or sisterly way, and that was all. My friends had no choice but to accept it and respect it.

Eventually Fire Starter (Steven) and I began to have a more solid friendship. We would always link up in pairs when we all hit the streets, and Steven would be hot on my heels. For some odd reason Steven was determined to go against the grain. He truly lived up to his name, Shit Starter—I mean Fire Starter. We began to kick it outside of our circle and started partying as a tag team. We attended family gatherings together and we went to straight clubs and NA meetings together (both of our parents were recovering addicts). It appeared we had a lot in common; while my dad was locked up in New York federal prison, his mother was too, for drug related charge. The more I expressed to Steven that I didn't like him like a boyfriend, the more he pressed the issue and the harder he would pursue me. He loved to brag to our friends how we went here or there together. He would share each outing in as much detail as possible.

On the other hand, I was trying to be careful not to create jealousy in our immediate circle. I could sense the jealousy, and Steven was feeding off the negative energy. I will admit it was amusing most of the time, because he was raw and didn't pull any punches when it came to the other Super Friends.

He would say to them, "Don't be jealous, and don't get mad because Chico (Tony) likes me more."

He was determined to ruffle some feathers by any means necessary. He started giving me a lot of money, usually in front of people. I would try to say no because I didn't want to encourage his sideshow, but he insisted. I knew he wasn't built like that but that didn't stop me from entertaining his facade. I rarely say no to money, but I knew he was acting like a dog and trying to mark his territory.

Eventually our friends raised eyebrows, getting suspicious, and one even made assumptions. But for every action there is always a reaction. My good friend Cobra Girl—I mean Cat Woman—(the snake of the crew) told someone that Steven and I were intimate, even after I made it clear that we never fucked or even kissed. The whole situation really hurt my feelings because he and I were friends longer than any of the other Super Friends. I had introduced him to the crew. I felt betrayed because he wanted to tarnish my name after I took him in when he had no place to go.

I was absolutely livid. To make matters worse, he said it behind my back. I went straight to the source and approached him. Cat Woman was stuttering on his words, and then he had the audacity to light a joint in my presence, like my concern didn't bother him. It was as if he was dismissing our whole conversation. I felt like he wanted to show off for our audience, so at that very moment I gave them a show. I begin to beat the shit out of him on his first inhale of his joint.

After I bloodied and bruised his face up, I stood over him and worked on his body. Then I picked up his phone, cracked him across the head, and told him, "Now call everybody and tell them how you got your ass whipped." Moments later we sat in complete silence, and my friends were in awe. Finally 'Taz' his lover at the time one of our mutual friends ran to his aid with a towel.

I lashed out, "Don't give him shit. This ass whipping was well overdue. Let his ass bleed," as I stood between the two of them.

I picked up his bag of weed, put it in my pocket, and grabbed his joint. Then I took a puff and took a seat.

I directed my attention back to Cat Woman, and then I said to him, "Now collect your thoughts, and tell me why you put a knife in my back again."

He couldn't answer me. He just buried his face in the sofa and cried.

I said to him, "Don't cry now, bitch. You should be preparing for your next report. This time you can spit some truth." Then I turned to everyone else and said, "I'm taking Steven home to fuck, and anyone who wants to pursue what's mine will get the same treatment." I looked at Cat Woman's lover and said, "Remind that bitch to never bring a knife to a gun fight."

After that night, Steven and I spent all of our spare time together, and he and I became a couple. In my mind I imagined Steven and I would get along well and grow together.

After dating for several months, he and I moved to his family's house and rented a room. The arrangement was comfortable. After a year into our relationship, we celebrated by having a one-year anniversary. A select few friends, his family, and of course, my family attended. Later as I looked back on the photos we took at the party, I noticed Steven was fucked up. Now considering we partied a lot—smoking weed and drinking—his addiction went unnoticed. In the past I had questioned why he would always get fucked up before me and why always to the fullest extent. We consumed the same amount of drinks and shared blunts. I never expressed my feelings with him;

I just assumed he had a low tolerance. After looking at the pictures, it confirmed my suspicions.

I immediately picked his brain for answers. I hoped he would come clean. I gave him every opportunity to share his struggle with me before I got gut-level honest and started being direct with him. I showed him the pictures and told him he was a dope fiend. He broke down and cried. He said he was sorry and he needed my help. I thought to myself, "Only GOD can help you now, and I need to gradually remove myself from this mess I jumped into headfirst."

For every question I asked, Steven had an answer. The only question he couldn't answer was why. When things were so good after over a year of sobriety, why would he pick up the habit again? He left me blindsided in the dark.

From the direction this conversation was going in, Steven must have figured my red flags were up and I was looking for the easiest route out. To my disadvantage Steven had always paid me a lot of attention; he enjoyed being the background to my foreground. He was prepared to handle me strategically, and at that moment our relationship began to feel like a crucial game of chess. Steven shared with me how he had struggled with his addiction since he was fifteen years old. He was very emotional, and his main concern was if I was going to leave him or not. My response to him was I needed to take a walk and clear my head. I just wanted to digest this situation and evaluate my life.

When I returned, blood was everywhere because he had slit his wrist. I rushed him to Sinai Hospital in Baltimore City, where they treated his wound and gave him a psychiatric evaluation. He was calm and patient and content with me at his side through the process. His peaceful disposition assured me this wasn't his first episode.

After all this drama hit me, I tried to leave him, but I had no one to share my problems with. I remember my mom would always say you can help people out sometimes, but usually they pull you down to their level. When I tried to leave him, I felt bad because I hate to kick a man when he's down. It was hard because my daily routine included him. I cared for him and enjoyed his company.

Steven wasn't giving up on our relationship. He would call constantly; he came to my job and my house just to talk to me.

I reasoned with myself, and thought everyone has some good in them, even if they constantly intentionally do wrong things. I thought to myself, "He needs my help. If he stayed clean that long once before, he can do it again." So I took him back.

When we got a new place together, I really paid attention and got to know the real Steven. I just saw him in a completely new light. He was conniving and sneaky and a con artist. He knew how to hustle. Despite discovering this, I felt our relationship was still pretty good. I never imagined he would direct that negative energy toward me.

Usually in my relationships I would spend all my time with my partner, and I was determined to keep this pattern with Steven. I found myself at malls while he stole handfuls of leather jackets, clothes, and purses. I was his lookout and I was usually driving the getaway car. I was on the strip while he sold stolen merchandise in exchange for money or drugs. He was determined not to allow me to go in the hole [alleys and side streets] while he copped his shit. He kept me in the hottest clothes and shoes. He kept himself looking decent too, for the most part. He started getting arrested and released on his own recognizance. It became obvious I was growing tired of our routine, but he knew if I was with you, I was really with you. Steven was well aware of my views and feelings about loyalty.

After a while common sense started to overshadow that character defect; my passion for loyalty. When we finally broke up, I left him with a vivid reminder of the past we created and the love we shared in the form of my nickname 'Chico' tattooed on his forearm. I wasn't so fortunate to escape with a simple tattoo. He gave me a gift that would stick with me for a life time. A gift I wouldn't give to a dying dog or my worst enemy, for that matter. I left with a newfound love for the most powerful *boy* in the world: heroin! In the streets, Boy is one of heroin's many known names, and crack is usually referred to as Girl.

I do take full responsibility for my addiction, but I also want to be as candid as possible when admitting that I do at times partially blame my ex-problem Steven. I blame him because he was a veteran in the drug game. He was also a lot older than I was, and he said and expressed that he loved me, so I trusted him. After we went back and forth about what it would feel like and how my body would react to the drug, Steven told me basically my body would reject the drug at first. He went on to describe the feeling to be like an extremely lengthy climax, and it would be the best high ever.

The first time I danced with the devil (heroin) and his advocate (Steven), it was on my twenty-fifth birthday. I was lying on my mother's living room floor, and I was asking—or better yet, ordering—Steven to give me some dope.

Steven sat beside me with a twenty-dollar bag of dope in one hand and a matchbook in the other. Even though we had no reason to rush because my family was out of town in Crownsville Maryland at a spiritual convention, I grew anxious because at this point my mind was made up. I wanted to feel *the greatest high ever*, just one time. Steven took a nickel coin and crushed the dope up on the end of the table while the dope was still in the bag. He then ripped the matchbook in half, leaving the end with no matches attached in his left hand while the bag of narcotics was still in his right hand.

I sarcastically lashed out, "Come on, baby," mimicking a scene from the legendary movie, *Lady Sings the Blues*, starring Diana Ross. I, of course, was Billie Holiday feigning for a hit, implying that Steven was Richard Pryor the piano man, providing the great white hope. We both laughed.

He looked at me with a straight face and said with a serious tone, "Chico, promise me you will never do this shit with anyone else."

I replied, "Boy, please."

He then said, "Please don't tell anyone I gave this to you, and, more importantly, promise me you'll never get hooked."

He stressed the seriousness of this particular drug, so I don't think he was intentionally trying to create a bad habit for me at the time. I am certain he was well aware that it was a strong possibility that I could very well become addicted.

Finally he dipped the matchbook corner in the bag of dope, pushed my left nostril close, and told me to sniff hard. We repeated the ritual with the left nostril. I had my first one-and-one, and I felt good. Steven then took a one-and-one for himself and watched me while my high took its course. I asked him why I tasted it in my mouth, and he told me that it was the drainage and not to spit it out but to just swallow.

We laugh and conversed for several minutes before I started to feel nauseous. As soon as he asked me if I felt sick, I instantly had to throw up. Without warning I ran to the bathroom.

I remember vomiting in the toilet on my knees while Steven held my individual plaits in one hand and massaged my back with his other hand. Steven said, "If you think you were high a minute ago, your ass is really going to feel good now."

He aided me to my feet, so I could brush my teeth and collect my thoughts. From the bathroom we went to the balcony to sit across from one another in the stylish wicker chairs while we smoked Newport's. I can't begin to describe this feeling. I felt happy and stress-free. My body felt light, and my brain wasn't racing. I was in complete bliss. I was just calm and at peace with myself and my surroundings. Steven and I continued to reminisce and laugh. Once again Steven demanded my full attention and reminded me how he looked and felt when he was ill from heroin. He stressed how I could never do this drug alone because three days in a row of heroin would definitely create a habit, and without a hit I would have a monkey on my back. He was clear and I understood.

Six months passed and I was still working to get high. Living in a two-bedroom apartment with Steven, I worked relentlessly to hide my addiction. I accepted the fact that I was a functioning addict and finally came to the realization that I needed help to fight this battle. I considered going to my mom for help, but I was afraid it would break her heart. My mom had been drug-free for several years and had left that memory in the past. It was my greatest wish to keep it just that: a bad memory from the past. Together we had struggled with that demon, and together we persevered. We had gone to meetings together and I visited and encouraged her when she went away. So I choose to withstand the rain and keep praying for a miracle.

The longer I indulged, the more my habit grew. I would cry myself to sleep at night praying for a second chance. It wasn't long before getting high was a top priority. Steven and I would cop drugs in the evening for the night, the morning after, and a small hit for a lunch special to carry us through the rest of the work shift. It graduated to the point where we would like to get high, but the primary goal was to cop drugs to at least feel normal. The high was an extra plus on a good day.

I wondered, "Is this a freak of nature?" I questioned myself because when it was time for my "medicine," my body would get hot, my stomach would knot up, and I would get very anxious. I was afraid to witness the beast at its fullest potential or that monkey on my back, so I was sure to obey when the desire surfaced. I stared aimlessly into the sky and thought to myself that since anything can happen, nothing should be considered freakish. I couldn't understand how a small bag of heroin the size of a pinky toenail could have complete control of a grown man's whole body and mind. I prayed for answers, for help, and above all I prayed for forgiveness.

Steven would question me, "Why you always get high and then want to pray?"

At one point I was in agreement. I thought maybe GOD wasn't listening. It was an underlying possibility that this was my future. In the past I was content and satisfied with the idea that I had a desire to sleep with men. I spoke to my GOD on many occasions, and finally I was assured that GOD didn't love me any less, and it was a desire I had no control over. I promised GOD and myself, if this was my path, I would walk it with respect. I wouldn't be loose or deceiving. I thought to myself that I'd rather choose a partner of the same sex rather than be a person who had multiple partners or sleep with more people than I had fingers. I found peace with myself and my GOD in that arena. Years later I had a serious drug addiction and a mate that challenged my faith and in turn influenced me to question my GOD.

Terry Lil' Bitts making money with a smile!

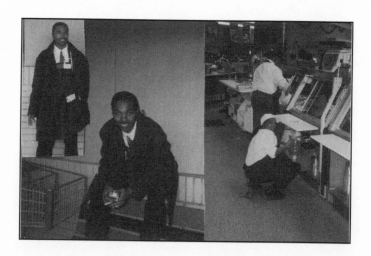

Terry and Tony at work

Tony Touch working at Safeway food market

CHAPTER 8

Perished And Flat Lined, But Too Young To Die

It was a cold night in January around 2:00 a.m. when Steven and I decided to make our way to Park Heights and Belvedere, our favorite strips to cop heroin. I favored PH because it was a familiar neighborhood and we knew all the top dog hustlers from selling clothes and shoes to them in exchange for money and drugs. I knew many nickel-and-dime corner boys from years of taking my unts and uncles across the tracks to cop drugs, well before I even started getting high. We also knew people in the neighborhood from school, and of course we knew other addicts and fiends. PH was close to home, and we were familiar with all the side streets and allies in the event we needed to shake the police.

There were always about six or seven shops open offering a variety of drugs on Park Heights. We would ask other addicts what's hot so we would get the most potent drugs or the biggest bags out at that particular time. It was a vicious cycle.

This was one rollercoaster I hoped would soon come to a sudden end. We had no desire to go out for anything other than drugs. Sometimes I had no appetite. I could go for days with no food as long as I had a hit.

When Steven and I got home, we sat in the center of the bed to split the product. He quickly collected his portion and retreated to the bathroom. I left him alone, took a hit, and laid back on the bed. I put Yolanda Adams's "The Battle Is Not Yours" on my CD player and tried to feed my spirit as I stared blankly at the ceiling.

A couple of days later, I told Steven, "I know what the deal is, so you no longer have to hide behind the bathroom door."

Steven had graduated—or should I say regressed back—to the old faithful spike [shooting up with the needle]. Steven's Aunt was a diabetic and received big bags of brand new needles on a monthly basis. Steven was at her house at the beginning of the month, like clockwork, to collect his fresh spikes. I witness Steven shooting his self up in Abandon homes, in people's back yards while I sniffed my heroin. It wasn't long before he was holding my arm, tying his belt around my forearm and shooting me up.

Being unemployed was not an option for me, I have worked my whole life since I was fifteen. I worked in high school, after high school, around the partying, and at that time to support my habit and pay the rent. In the morning Steven and I worked with my mother in Owings Mills at the Safeway Food Market. Steven and I also worked at a townhouse on Liberty Heights and Gwynne Oak on Mondays, Wednesdays, and Fridays from 11:00 p.m. until 7:00 a.m. assisting six mentally retarded adult patients.

My very first time trying the needle was during a shift at the group home. I overdosed and woke up to paramedics surrounding me on the floor. I never knew how long I was flat-lined, but the Lord felt it was not my time to go yet. At this juncture, I viewed my life as worthless, without value. I stood to my feet with an overwhelming headache, and instantaneously the paramedics spotted me as I sat on the bed.

Several strangers stood around me, talking. I heard someone whisper, "He doesn't have any track marks, and there are no needles."

Steven was standing in the bathroom doorway, towering down and witnessing the whole situation. While he answered one paramedic's questions, Steven made eye contact with me, basically saying to act like I was unaware of my surroundings and unwilling to answer any questions. We spoke without words. Steven was truly a veteran in this drug game.

It had been such a long time since my mind and body was completely drug-free. The paramedics injected me with a medication to bring me back to consciousness and cleanse my system. It made me reject the narcotics in my system, causing me to feel sick. I sat on the bed and wondered why they hadn't let me just die. I was so confused, and I wondered why anyone would want to go on living in this state. Was there ever going to be an end to this madness?

I sat feeling sorry for myself and tried to recall the tragic events from the time I consumed the dope, but the memory was foggy and unclear to me. Just as the paramedics quickly packed their equipment, I started to feel ill. Moments after they left our work site, I ran to the bathroom assisted by Steven. I threw up and had to defecate.

All the drugs were gone, but Steven still had the empty bag of dope. He put a little water in the bag and told me to suck the bag to consume the entire residue. To my surprise, it gave me a slight sense of relief. He suggested I wait there with the patients while he traveled across the tracks to get some drugs so I could get out of the gate [get heroin to relieve the pain].

I replied, "Hell no. I'm going to get my own dope. We can go together, or you can stay your ass here."

As we walked toward Garrison Boulevard to get a hack [illegal taxi] to the strip, I asked Steven what exactly happened when I passed out after he gave me a hit. He said I stood to my feet after he untied the belt from my arm, and then seconds later I fell backwards onto the floor and I was completely unconscious. He said he tried to revive me and instantly called 911 from the neighbor's house. He said he sat with me and continued to try to wake me up.

When the paramedics arrived, he went out the back door and came in the front door behind the paramedics, acting like he had just gotten there. He then explained to me that if he was found with me, he could be arrested and they could try to pin a murder charge on him. I had heard something to that effect in the past.

Then he laughed and tried to make light of the situation. He said, "You know, if our bosses come in and the patients are home alone, we are going to get fired."

I replied, "Then their asses won't have anyone to watch their patients."

He agreed and added, "And they will have to explain why they authorized me to distribute medication on a daily basis with no license."

I didn't really trust the married couple we worked for under the table: They always wanted us to stop by the house to distribute meds and feed the patients on our off days, because we lived near the work site. Our pay was always late and we had to debate in regards to the overtime payments, only because we were expected to do over time as a favor. They expressed that they used to hang in the gay clubs together over ten years ago. They would stress how they were familiar with the local gay bars here in Baltimore like; Hippo, Paradox, Marty Gross, The Eagle, and the Club Buns. Most of these places with the exception of a select few were nothing to brag about; in fact if I cared, I would have advise them to never volunteer that information again, because people places and things say a lot about a man's character. They where even well versed in Alga [a rare gay language similar to Pig Latin]; Move the onset of the first syllable to the end of each word, and add "alga" to the end of each word. When I learned that they mastered Alga that instantly made me suspicious. I was familiar with people sharing their encounters with the gay society to get in good, to feel a part of it, or to earn favor in my eyes, but this was extremely different. This wasn't a situation where four ordinary people were just having a normal conversation that happened to be about homosexuality, the lifestyle, or just past experiences. This was a reoccurring conversation. I was certain the husband had a hidden agenda, and he didn't put much effort into keeping it hidden. He made bold advances at me, to the extent where his wife was in the other room with Steven.

Sometimes he would give me extra money on pay day and after he put the inaccurate amount in my hand he would stare at me in a lustful manner. Steven would encourage me to burn his pockets up every time he saw me. I was certain if he was that aggressive with me, he wouldn't hesitate to make advances at Steven, so I was very alert and on point in his presence. I made Steven fully aware of the situation, and he said he knew and it was cool. I felt bad for his wife, but Steven assured me she was well aware of his fantasies.

I could sense Steven was angry with both the husband and wife. I was ready to quit, but Steven had other plans in mind. The arrangement with the husband and Steven was short-lived, and it wasn't long before Steven gave the couple an ultimatum. Either they would give him a large sum of money in addition to our pay, or he would expose the couple's illegal practices and their crafty business affairs.

They were collecting several checks on the behalf of dead patients, which came in the mail to the townhouse we worked in. The couple was committing tax fraud in addition to other illegal stunts.

When the confrontation first started, Steven exposed the husband to the wife. After that, they didn't want to test Steven because it was evident he had no conscience. I, on the other hand, was completely silent and baffled. This confrontation was a long battle that went on for a couple of hours but it seemed like forever. We sat in the living room where we worked: Steven, the husband, his wife, and me, while the patients all stayed upstairs. There was so much tension in the air you could cut it with a knife. Steven and the husband debated and argued back and forth while the wife and I sat silently and watched the fire escalate.

At one point she tried to go in on Steven. She was telling him he'd better leave her house, and she warned me that I should leave Steven alone, because he wasn't worth shit. She even tried to deny her husband's advances. Steven gave her the same treatment: no respect. And everything she spat at him, he shut it down and made her eat her words.

Steven then looked at me with rage in his eyes and said, "Chico didn't he try to show you his dick?"

I replied, "Yes, he did," in a confident yet sarcastic tone.

Steven looked at her and told her, "You know what the fuck is going on. You'd rather him push up on me or Tony so you can account for his where-abouts. That option beats him chasing some shit on the streets while you don't have a clue who he's sleeping with and what type of diseases they are carrying. You figure you'd rather gamble with us 'cause it's not likely he'll be here getting any play, because we are always together. And if so, it wouldn't be an ongoing affair, because time won't allow it. It would be more like a hit and miss from time to time."

Then and only then did I agree with Steven when he said "She knew what was going on," her reaction told it all.

She shouted "leave my house."

Steven said, "If you want me to leave, call the police, 'cause I got a story to tell. Or give me my fucking money, because I'm not playing with ya'll."

I took Steven to the side, and we conversed while our bosses discussed how to get out this shit they were now knee deep in. I suggested that we leave and set a time and day to come back to get our pay and the money Steven was blackmailing them for. I just wanted to get the fuck away from there.

Steven said, "No, baby, please trust me. They got money in the bank, and they are wrong, so please just chill. You don't have to say or do anything. Just stay here with me." Steven made it clear to me that if we left and set a day to pick up our pay, we would never receive it.

Months later, I saw the wife, and we said a cordial hello to one another. Our greeting seemed sincere, and the look in her eyes asked me for forgive-ness. When we passed one another again in the market, she built up enough nerve to ask me if I was still dating Steven, and I responded no. She gave me a hug and apologized for me being caught in the middle and wished me luck.

I told her I would keep her in my prayers. I thought to myself, I pray we don't cross paths again. A part of me wanted to ask her, "Are you still married to that trash you introduced me to?" But it was not the Christ-like thing to do, plus I already knew the answer, because I saw him drop her off at the main entrance.

Eventually Steven got arrested, and just like always I supported him. He was sent to Towson Detention Center, a no-contact facility. Steven educated me on how to fully support him and his habit while he served his time; I was printing self-addressed envelopes with the lawyer's mailing address and information. I copied legal documents from the attorney and stapled a bag of dope in the top left-hand corner to be certain the narcotics would go unnoticed when the letter was put through the e-ray machine at the facility. Steven told me the correctional officers opened and checked all the incoming and outgoing mail, but it was against the law to open any legal documents from an attorney. When he was transferred to the Department of Corrections pre-release center in Jessup MD, I carried drugs under my tongue and passed them with a kiss. I sent packages, money and I even visited on a regular basis.

I was a complete ass for so long. When Steven was released, things went back to the regular routine.

One day I came home from work and told Steven I had to move back home. Steven cried and told me he had been in love with me well before we started dating. He told me how strong I was, how he loved everything about me. He commented on my thick eyebrows, my long eyelashes, and the way I danced. He praised me and pleaded with me.

I stood firm and spoke to him with conviction. "Steven, I'm sorry, but I want to get clean."

He tried to scare me with suicidal threats of killing his self, if I left.

He was desperate and promised me we could go to a recovery house together. I didn't think he would follow through with the threats of killing his self but I must admit it softened my heart a little. I pounder with the idea of staying, while I squinted I studied his eyes for his hidden truth. To seal the deal, I called my mother for support, guidance and also to send Steven a subliminal message. Steven got the hint; he was convinced I was serious because it had always been more vital than anything to keep this addiction from my mother. It was more essential to me to hide the truth from my mother to spare her the pain and heartache. Keeping this secret from her was more imperative than my longing and my greatest desire to get clean.

Of course she came right over to my aid. After she arrived, we took a ride together and just conversed. When I finally built up enough nerve to tell her what the problem was, we cried together, and she held me in her arms. She wanted to know why no one told her what was going on with me, and how when we saw so much of one another the addiction still went unnoticed. At the time we all worked together at Safeway in different departments; me, my mother, and Steven (whom my mother loathed.) I explained that I made it clear to my family that she wasn't to find out about my addiction under any circumstances.

Naturally my mom expressed that she wanted to have Steven done in [shot]. She vented that a head went for fifty dollars in the hood, but her primary concern was her baby. She had to verbally pray aloud and be mindful that Steven was still one of GOD's creations and some ones baby as well. I felt the indescribable heart wrenching agony she was experiencing, just by looking in her eyes and hearing her express herself in that fashion. I felt so bad to disappoint her and cause her so much pain. Especially considering she was just warming up to the idea that her only son was a bi-sexual, but I didn't have a choice in the matter, I really needed her help.

I believe most parents go through a similar process when they suddenly find out their child may not be able to achieve the American dream or bless them with grand children. I would imagine the idea of your child readily facing judgment, harassment or just simply being mistreated is an overwhelming thought. It is imperative to give parents time to mourn the death of the baby they once knew, to grieve for the dreams they may have once had for their child's future. Certainly every parent has high hopes and big dreams for their children. Being mindful I just told my mother about my life style within the recent years, I wanted to be extra careful not to drop any sudden bombs on her because a person can only take so much before they go off. I've learned that people are like pipes; if you apply too much pressure on them, overtime they will explode and in some cases they rupture suddenly with no warning. To my surprise she could handle more than I gave her credit for. My mother actually handled the situation like a champ, because a mother's strength and love is usually discredited but undoubtedly unmatched.

On September 11, 2001, Steven and I woke up to cop some drugs in enough time for me to be back so my mom could pick me up for a scheduled trip to a thirty-day rehab facility called "Right Turn". The news broadcast announced there was an attack on the Twin Towers in New York City. The broadcast aired the footage over and over again. It was so vivid and so real. I just cried for the victims and the families affected. I was also crying because I felt like I was the Twin Towers crashing to the ground and causing nothing but pain and misery to all my loved ones.

Two weeks after I went away to rehab, Steven came and admitted himself into the same facility. When I graduated from the program, it wasn't long before I started using again, which was around the time Steven was scheduled to graduate. He had continued the program for live-in outpatient treatment. The stipulations required live-in patients to submit urine samples once a week, they had to be in before the ten o'clock curfew, and finally patients had to renew their residency every six months. It only made sense considering Steven burned every bridge he crossed. He had absolutely nowhere to go— not even his family members supported or trusted him. He was restricted to do random urine drug test and his reward was the privileged to stay at the facility for free housing for the homeless.

I was living back home, so He and I made plans to meet up. Better judgment urged me to cop before we met and keep my business just that, my business. Loyalty, respect and the burdens of habit dominated my decision. When we met up, I explained to him that I had relapsed and I needed to go cop and he had to wait, because I didn't want to jeopardize his sobriety or entice him. My logic said it was okay to get high because I was only sniffing blow [Heroin] every couple of days, but reality was I was playing with my sobriety, my life, and I was "living in confusion" [Phyllis Hyman].

Even after I relapsed I was still attempting to show Steven and his recovery process a certain level of respect. I was simply being honest by handling my transactions before I saw him, trying to be proactive to prevent the urge from surfacing on my account. Steven told me that we needed to make plans to go to the movies another day because he didn't want to wait while I copped drugs. I felt that if that was the case, he didn't have to be so forward and mean. He could have softened the blow. I thought about all the times I accompanied him to different strips [areas in which to purchase drugs], waited for him to cop, and swept his addiction under the rug. I had been drug-free all those times in the past when we copped drugs and although I was tuff, I was obviously green to the drug game. Unlike in the past Steven didn't spare me his venom and our next exchange would determine whether my wit and strength could match his venom.

I felt the built-up anger and hatred for him surface. It was as if I could feel the heat from my feet rise to my eyebrows. I was in a complete rage, and my first instinct was to beat the shit out of him. But I built up enough strength to walk away. It was hard to walk away because I wanted to defend myself, but I learned many things from some familiar scriptures to help navigate me out of this bad situation. To my surprise the scriptures only made me more confused, because often I have to take time to internalize the words full and complete meaning to understand GOD's instructions. — **2 Timothy 3:7, 2 Timothy 3:16** [refer to chapter 11]

I wanted to remain obedient and allow GOD to defend me and my honor is his own time. For me that was the most challenging test of my struggles. I was accustomed to leaving people where they are, but I put a lot of time and energy in avoiding my enemies, because I know my potential and I know what I was taught. I always imagined by staying away from my adversary, I was being kind and docile. —**Romans 12:17-21** [refer to chapter 11]

I kept thinking to myself he is like a lion and he wants to conquer my spirit and tear at my flesh. —**1ˢᵗ Peter 5:8-11** [refer to chapter 11]

I felt like an Elephant defending his territory from a threat, that's really no threat; the well known king of the jungle, the Lion vs. the real deal the underestimated Elephant. —**Ecclesiastes 3:7-8** [refer to chapter 11]

While I was struggling with how I was going to respond to him in a Christ like manner, he said in a sarcastic tone, "Chico, you might wanna think about going with me to an NA meeting." It was clear that he wanted to embarrass and belittle me or just simply get a response from me, so I turned to face him and grabbed his dreads with a death-lock grip. I pulled him down to the ground with my left hand, while I gripped his dreads with all my strength. I continued to bang him with my right fist. When he finally grabbed the light pole for support, he reached up to grab my hair, and I snatched his head back down to the ground and continued to pound on him. When I let go of his dreads, I found I had ripped a big patch of hair out of the center of his head. He was unable to defend himself and was in complete shock.

I waited for him to redeem himself and gave him an opportunity to defend his honor, but he only screamed out, "Look what you did to my face! What is wrong with you?"

He stood up and was hurt physically and emotionally. More than anything, his pride was crushed. Strangers stood around and were shocked that my five-foot-seven ass could dominate his six-foot-two ass with so much ease.

When our eyes connected, I replied to his shouts. "I didn't do that to your face. You did, when you played on my intelligence and took my kindness for weakness."

When I turned to walk away, Steven tried to throw his weight on me by charging me and grabbing me from behind. I instantly spun around, leaving him standing with just my jacket in his hands. I kicked Steven in his chest. He fell back to the ground, looking up at me from his back while he kicked wildly in attempts to connect. As our audience formed, I quickly grew tired of his pointless attempts to kick me, so I picked up a brick and told him if he kicked at me again, I was going to bust his shit to the white meat.

He curled up in the fetal position and said between sobs, "I'm sorry, I'm sorry."

I threw the brick far from his reach, picked my jacket up, and left him lying on the sidewalk in front of Rogers's subway station along with his audience he was determine to entertain.

One day some of our mutual friends, who were also functional addicts, went to cop [purchase drugs] with me. We got high and played catch up. They told me they heard about the fight. To my surprise they had a pretty accurate report. The tale proved the streets are always watching and the streets are always talking [Jay Z]. We laughed and I asked how Steven was doing.

Someone said, "You know Steven, don't you?"

That statement confirmed that he was still getting high. I'm sorry to admit, but a feeling of joy took over my spirit. They went on to say how he constantly claimed he was going to get me back, and the only reason I beat his ass was because he couldn't bring himself to hit me.

I fell over laughing and said, "He always had a vivid imagination. You know he was an only child, right?" Before we ended the conversation about the number one stunner [fraud], they shared that he was forced to cut his hair bald because I ripped a patch of his dreads out of the crown of his head. I was glad and amused and I said "well at least he's tall so it won't be too noticeable while he's out copping' and bopping'.

When I got home to my Grandmother Marilyn's house, I grabbed some fruit and set on DJ Grannies bed and shared a censored version of the highlights of my day. Between narratives and stories granny became relaxed and started to fall asleep. Unaware: I was worrying, and inducing restless nights on both my grandmothers and my mother. When she fell asleep I kissed her on the head and quickly retreated to my room, pulled my stash out of the closet, and proceeded to fulfill a long-held desire to successfully shoot up. I thought this event through thoroughly and decided to inject myself in the ankle to prevent from making a mark on my arm. I promised myself this would be the one and only time I would shoot up, considering the first time with Steven had not been successful. It was a vague memory, but what was vivid in my mind was the real good feeling of the high that hit me instantaneously.

I proceeded to calmly crush my dope; I put the dope on the spoon and added a needle capful of water. I completed my task by putting a lighter under the spoon to make my liquid poison. I carefully injected myself in the ankle. I never bothered to tie the belt around my leg. When the blood from the vein hit the syringe, I immediately emptied the needle of heroin into my system.

Instantly the heroin took over my body. I was so high that words couldn't begin to express what I felt. My bedroom door was shut, and the music played sweet sounds of Anita Baker's "Only for a While."

Once again I had overdosed. This time it was clearly a miracle I was found. I'm not sure if my grandmother found me herself or she sent my favorite Aunt Octavia (Yoddy) who's mildly mentally challenged to check on me. I truly believe GOD sent a portion of his Holy Spirit and guided my grandmother to my aid.

My Grandmother Marilyn's home was peaceful. She was well aware of my actions and prayed for my deliverance. However, she didn't hassle me, mistreat me, or belittle me for my disease of addiction. She still respected me and my space. It wasn't likely that she would travel three flights of stairs in the middle of the night, but to my surprise, she would check on me throughout the night when her spirit would move her.

When I woke up after the overdose, I was being wheeled on a gurney in Northwest Hospital. My family was all around the bed, crying and praying for me to live. My sight was blurry and I couldn't hear at all. My vision was slowly returning but the bright lights were overpowering, and I remember my mother holding my hand, crying and trying to smile to keep me calm.

I vividly remember looking into her tearful eyes and trying to say to her, "Everything is okay, Mom. I'm all right," but I couldn't speak.

Everyone was crying and screaming. After a few moments, my hearing started to gradually come back, but I was still unable to speak. So I just focused on my mom, and I could literally see myself in her tearful eyes. I could see all the machines the doctors had me hooked up to. It truly felt like an out-of-body experience. I was well aware of my surroundings, but I was unsure about how I got there and what put me in this predicament.

When my grandmother grabbed my other hand and gently kissed my forehead, my heart broke; everything was made clear to me. I could recall being in her home when I overdosed, and I imagined that she had found me. I imagined all the pain I caused her, knowing how much she cared for me and how she expected so much more from her protégé.

I spent seven days in the hospital, during which my grandmothers, my aunts; Pat, Kat and Yoddy came to visit me every day. My mother stayed by my side the whole time. Frog was there, he made rounds to my mom's house to get clothes for my mother and to also drive my grandmother Barbara back and forth to the hospital. The rest of the family would visit daily and rotate shifts. This was truly my breaking point. I took that week to think about the year I spent using drugs, getting high, and slowly killing not just myself but the ones who meant the world to me: my family.

I wondered how I would ever repay my family for all the love and support they showed me while I was damaging myself and hurting my loved ones. I had created nothing but stress and pain for them. I also found that while most of my family loved me through my mess, there were a select few that shared my struggles with the streets. I couldn't understand how anyone within the family could have felt comfort in my moments of confusion. Later it all became clear some people just have jealous hearts and operate out of spite. Usually those types of people simply feel joy when they witness or inflict pain on others. I realized the best way to fix things was to clean up what I messed up and start fresh, because twenty-five was just too young to die.

Tony and Mark out on the town

CHAPTER 9

Facing And Defeating The Man In The Mirror

- program called "I Can't We Can," I began to set short-term and long-term goals and focus on completing them. Above all things I wanted to strengthen my relationship with my GOD and hopefully develop a fear of displeasing GOD. I was aware that I served a kind and forgiving GOD, and I knew he would continue to forgive me. I wanted to graduate from the program with success this time, I wanted to go to school, obtain a job, and finally work my way into management. Long-term goals were also made to be achievable. I wanted to complete a real-estate course and hopefully purchase my first single-family home, adopt a child, write a book, replace my dream car (the Acura I lost in a bad relationship), and finally give love one more chance.

I went to computer school, where I graduated and earned my certificate, and from there I started a new job at Whole Foods Market as a front end cashier. It was only a few months before I worked my way into management, because I was finally learning to love myself again. I recognized the things I had ignored about myself for so many years. I took a profound look at myself and found many things I wanted to change. I had a short fuse and I was often violent, I was bossy, I held grudges, and I was very vindictive. I was a people pleasure to the degree of default. In the process of this growth, I allowed myself to let go and let GOD, and it worked. I changed and saw a major improvement.

I'm well aware that I'm human, so backslides are possible, but I have evolved into a positive young man, and I'm not likely to be set back so easily today. My mother always reminds me the Bible says a righteous man may fall up to seven times, but he still gets up. GOD sends people to help make us become the person he created us to be. We need to take notice and embrace our gifts. In the process we must also be aware of wolves dressed in sheep's clothing. I finally gave myself a chance, a chance to be a better me.

My family attended the program meetings and came to Goofy Friday and the dances every week. I recall my mother's words of encouragement in my time of doubt: "Stand tall, my love."

Three months later, I completed the program and was promoted to a front end supervisor in customer service on my job. My mother found me a new car, so she and my old acquaintance Gerald pitched in and purchased the Honda Civic, and I was overjoyed.

It seemed like so many people were interested in me, but I was so distant, and a relationship was supposed to be the last focus on my priority list. Life was good, but I was missing companionship, and being a relationship-oriented person made me feel it even more. I was in the habit of being in a relationship. I always believed being in a relationship helped preserve me and kept me stable and out of trouble. It wasn't until I lived a little that I realized that playing house could also work against me even more than it had helped me in the past. I would go out occasionally and feel like a celebrity for that moment, and that was almost like a high to me. It was validating and confirming.

One night my Aunt Pat (my road dog) and I were out on the town, and Mark approached me. He asked me what was wrong and what could he do to help me. I was shocked he knew me well enough to see through the mask I faithfully resorted to in my time of despair. Undoubtedly I was apprehensive about sharing my thoughts and issues. I never really was a talker but more of a thinker. I spent a lot of time up in my head. I was in the habit of resolving my problems by helping others address their issues. That tactic was helpful, but it never really got to the core of my issues.

After a while of simply being patient and determined, Mark was able to break through. He brought issues of mine to the surface I wasn't even aware I was struggling with. I tried to redirect our conversation, but he handled me with care. He was careful not to pry or pressure me but he allowed his genuine concern for me to dominate our conversation.

To prove his sincerity, he then pulled out his wallet and said to me, "I never stop carrying this picture of you, and I never took this ring off because I knew you would return to me."

I laughed and thought he was joking.

He looked into my eyes and said, "You don't want to be in here The Sportsmen's hole in the wall bar. You are cut from a different cloth. Let me take care of you." Marks words pierced my soul, and demanded my full attention for a brief moment.

Mark and I enjoyed our time together that night, but it was clear I wasn't taking his conversation seriously. When it was obvious to Mark that Aunt Pat and I found humor in his attempt to express his feelings, he excused himself and exchanged words with the bartender. When Mark returned, he brought Aunt Pat and me another drink of Hennessy and Coke.

Moments later the karaoke screen lit up, and Mark sang me a song, "Just Once," by James Ingram. I tried to remain still in an effort not to draw any more unwanted attention to myself, but my efforts were pointless because the spotlight was literally on the three of us.

As the night went on, Aunt Pat and Mark dominated the karaoke microphones, singing duets and solos until we left the club.

Before the night came to an end, Mark got right back to the subject he started during our initial encounter at the bar; he remembered exactly where we started and where stopped in the beginning of our reencounter. My jaw dropped and I told Mark we could talk about that later.

Once we got back to my house, he finally persuaded me to open up and let him in. He was able to break my pride. He assured me that he would respect me no matter what my issues were. He told me if I couldn't face my problem, I would never be able to fix my problem. I reluctantly broke my silence and expressed myself to him. I confessed that I used to get high, and I didn't think much of myself. I felt as though I had wasted too much time and would never get back on track or in a position to fulfill all my dreams.

I told him I was incapable of loving someone outside my family in an intimate way. Mark wasn't taken aback by my confessions; it was almost like he was even more drawn to me.

Mark asked, "Do you care for me?"

I replied, "Of course I do," as I wiped my tears and buried my head on his shoulders.

Mark embraced me, and I felt safe, desired in spite of my flaws, and above all I felt loved.

He said, "I love you Tony, and my uncle told me if you love something, hold on to it, and eventually it won't have a choice but to love you back."

That was the first time I felt loved with no stipulations or expectations attached, I felt loved for just the price of love in return.

Aunt Pat, Mark, and I lived together for almost two years, and we had the time of our life. We partied, constantly cooked, drank, attended church regularly and were all dedicated members of the church choir. At my church Scripturally Sound I felt my feet where planted on solid soul, which made learning and fellowshipping a true joy. We had family reunions and family functions at The Ranch (Aunt Pat's house).

A few years later, my cousin Tamia got married, and she and I had a conversation about how she felt unsure about her new union. It became obvious to me she needed my support. The marriage became violent and abusive. It wasn't long before Tamia, her children, her husband, Mark, and I moved, with the attempts to purchase our first house together.

I was happy with my job as a supervisor at Whole Foods Market; however, I was looking to move toward my career in real estate. In 2006 my cousin suggested I apply with the company she worked for as a leasing agent on a different property, and it was the perfect fit. I got a chance to exercise my customer service skills and work a normal nine-to-five shift.

After a year in our apartment, we attempted to purchase a row house. My cousin, Tamia and I rented the row house with an option to buy after the first year. Although the house was structured to meet all of our needs, my cousin and I were indecisive about making that long-term commitment.

In the end we decided to move out after the first year of renting, we moved into our Aunt Kat's single-family detached home in Baltimore County. It was then that I realized that for over a year I was legally considered homeless. My name wasn't even on the lease for the town home I was previous residing in with the intent to buy. However, this decision to move into aunt Kat's house was a better arrangement because it allowed us the luxury of a full front and back fenced in yard. The home was centrally located where all our family could attend our family functions.

After the first year of occupying aunt Kat's home, my Cousin and my Aunt could not find a common ground. Any simple matter was ignited to a full-blown argument, and I found myself being the referee for two grown women I loved and respected. Not only were the two women at each other's throats but the negative energy began to hinder the solid bond between my cousin and me, which assured me that our season was coming to an end.

Eventually I could sense that the arrangement was putting a strain on my relationship with Mark, who was ready to move and start our own family. I couldn't relate to his desire to take the next step in our relationship. I was comfortable with my extended family because the children brought us a lot of joy. I felt his relationship was so strong with Tamia and the kids, I never considered that he just wanted us to grow and extend our own family. I was blind to the big picture, and I was also afraid. Afraid of change and scared to make that commitment with just him and I alone, because in the past that decision brought me pain and turmoil, not just once but on numerous occasions.

For the past two years, Mark had been working at a popular funeral home. During the day Mark would dress the bodies up, and conduct funerals, while I worked for a real-estate company. He and I would pick bodies up, and take them to the funeral home at night. It was a good job and something new for me to experience, and who better to experience it with than the man I loved. Mark was a good talker so he persuaded the owner to put me on the payroll. The job required two people to collect the bodies in homes, and one person to abstract a body from the hospitals or nursing homes.

After four years Mark lost the job, it was a major adjustment for me financially, but I was certain unemployment would carry Mark's weight until he found work. I was taken back when I realized the household had a strong desire for Mark to move. Inside my home everyone was tense, and that was an uncommon cycle in our home. It was usually happy and peaceful. One day my cousin and I had a heated argument, and she reminded me that I could always leave. When the words registered, I blew my cool and my pitch switched gears. I said some mean things in reply to her suggestion and left her standing upset and in tears. Later I cried to Mark, prayed about it and the answer to my prayers became clear. I then decided to step out on faith, and within a week Mark and I rented an apartment home in Owings Mills from the corporation I was employed with. Before I left, my cousin and I parted on good terms, and several months later she moved in the same complex, and our relationship continued to grow. Mark and I apartment was only minutes away from my mom, Terry. We spent a lot of time together and with my mom, and that too brought me a lot of joy.

Although I was afraid to move in the beginning, I am thankful, because many of my long-term goals were being fulfilled. Mark and I completed the foster care course and waited to welcome our new child home. My mom also completed the foster care back-up course and earned her certificate. I was finally completing my book, I was building my credit as well as my Beacon score, and I had high hopes of purchasing my first home.

Looking back now, I truly see how you can be your biggest cheerleader and yet your worst enemy. My primary goal then and today is to stay focused, remain encouraged, and develop the necessary tools to defeat the man in the mirror. In essence I must stay aware and be prepared for adversities and hidden distractions outside as well as within my immediate circle.

Robert, Mark, Justin, and Tony @ a cook out

CHAPTER 10

Giving Up

Self-doubt acts as a cage and puts you in a mental prison stagnating you from growth. This state of mind surfaces the forefront of my mind at my weakest hour. At times it consumed my thoughts and aspirations. I questioned my ambition and goals only to find myself frustrated and discouraged. I felt like so much time had passed, and yet I hadn't adopt a child, published my first book, or started the process of buying my own home.

I remember sitting in a hot tub surrounded with scented candles, listening to Lalah Hathaway (*Self Portrait album*) and thinking to myself, "It would be so easy to just give up. Stop trying to overachieve because I felt I'm just overwhelming myself." I begin to think maybe I was meant to maintain a stable job, stay out of trouble, and just work to pay bills. Maybe the American dream was a distraction from my path.

I could hear Mark speaking through the door. "Stinky, are you okay?"

I replied sourly, "Yes, I'm fine." I could hear genuine concern in his voice, but I didn't have the strength to pacify anyone at that moment or appear strong. For that instant, I allowed his mind to wonder.

After about five minutes, he returned to the door to say, "Your phone is ringing. Do you want me to answer it?"

I thought to myself, "Throw it over the balcony." I assumed he had called my mom to make her aware that I was not in good spirits and he didn't know which route to take to ease my discomfort. Or it was a family member or a friend being needy, and I couldn't even fulfill my own needs at the time.

To my surprise it was Social Services. They wanted me to meet a ten-year-old child who needed housing. My initial intent was to adopt a child between the ages of two and five years old, but the Social Services worker gave me an extremely brief description of this innocent's child's story, and I was moved. I agreed to meet him the next day after work at my home.

After the social worker, Mark, my Mom, and I met the child, Doodle, I was torn. I was trying to stay on track with my original plan to adopt a younger child.

When Doodle first entered our home, he was not what I imagined, and I was certain this was a temporary arrangement. Once we made eye contact, the silent conversation challenged my beliefs. I saw a lost child full of disappointment, fear, and pain. When I sized him up and down, at that very moment my heart broke, and I wanted to hold him in my arms and assure him that everything would be okay. Better judgment suggested I pray and be still. He was ten years old and came only with the shirt on his back. He had several holes in his shoes, a pair of dirty shorts, and a holey T-shirt. He didn't have any underclothes, socks, or a jacket. I recall thinking to myself; although I set a goal to care for a child between the ages of two and five, maybe GOD had a different plan for me and my family.

After Doodle and I made eye contact, the conversation was profound. I could sense his pain and struggle. That silent conversation answered many questions, but it was important that he verbalized his wants and needs.

At that moment I felt compelled to speak, so I introduced Mark, my Mom, and myself to him. I asked him one question: "Do you want to stay here?"

I was forced to determine his future based on his simple answer of yes or no.

He was fascinated with my best friend, Queen Annie, my little Cockapoo. I shared with Doodle how my intent was to save her life, but she was the one that saved my life instead. Annie lifted my spirits and gave me hope when I was in a very delicate state of mind, and she has been a part of our family every since. When I noticed he was intrigued by the history of how Queen Annie came to be. In that moment the life lessons began and I went on by sharing how she was abandoned in one of my scheduled evictions for almost a week before we rescued her.

In front of an half open balcony door, Annie laid cold, hungry with no food, and no water locked in a cage. Queen Annie wasn't even left with a night light to calm her fears. She was left along with unwanted furniture, dirty clothes and with no electricity. She was weak and malnourished and reeked of her own bowels and urine. I ashoared him she wasn't nearly as attractive as she is today. When my property manager discovered her she immediately called me to see if I could locate the original owners to see if I could persuade them to retrieve her. Together we called the residents and they refused to pick her up, so my manager offered her to me. Doodle understood the point and the underlined message; He knew that we loved and adored Queen Annie (Puddin'). He understood that you never know where your help can come from. Love has no boundaries, it's color-blind, and everyone is deserving of love.

After a few hours in our home, Doodle bathed and prepared himself for dinner. We spent a lot time getting to know one another. Doodle (Dew), Mark (Stinky), Terry (Ma), and I were all cautious, yet curious. I could appreciate him and his beauty, and he was utterly appreciative to be with us as well. Doodle spent a while in the tub and surfaced looking like he felt relieved from a long journey across the Judean Desert. Terry and Mark had completed dinner, and I prepared the plates and set the table. We settled down and blessed our meal. It was a great union. We sat for over an hour just talking, laughing, and becoming familiar.

It was challenging in the beginning trying to instill the basic morals and values a young man spends most of his youth learning. Doodle, on the other hand, was a people pleaser, and he had a natural desire to do well and please those he felt loved and cared for him. Although, he had been raised and taught how to live in the dark, being manipulative and sneaky to get ahead. I was certain I had my hands full. I felt like I had a late start with Doodle and for that we were the underdogs destined to succeed. I did everything possible to be sure Doodle received a fair chance. I was also trying to wash away his past by providing nothing but the best for him and expecting nothing but the best from him.

Time has been an awesome revealer, and time allowed me to see just how resilient he is. Coupled with his big mouth, because he was far from shy, Doodle would speak whatever entered his mind, just totally out of order, but with good intentions. Doodle had a hard walk and he was exposed to things that even as adults we can't imagine how we could stay focused on the light at the end of the tunnel.

Some of his paths harden my heart, but they also encourage me to persevere and stay focused. I stay focused not only for GOD and myself, but for him too. I now have one more boulder on my shoulder forcing me to lead by example and do the right thing. I am amazed how a child with so much pain, turmoil, and loss can still project that joy with an innocent, childlike demeanor. Doodle still enjoys life and has trust in adults and embraces this new life with ease.

After we registered Doodle into Baltimore County public school, weeks passed and he asked if he could call me dad. I was overjoyed and honored. I sensed the tension Mark felt by being labeled uncle and me, on the other hand, as Doodle's dad, and Terry as his mom-mom. I found myself assuring Mark that things would work them-selves out and with time I would explain the full picture to Dew. I just felt we needed to follow protocol and not volunteer any extra confusion to this complicated yet delicate family. After awhile I thought maybe Doodle could call him pop or something similar, but by that time, Mark and Doodle had embraced the title Uncle Mark. We all understood that we are both his dad in our own right. It was evident that Mark was indeed Dad material and any stranger could recognize that both Mark and I both fulfill that role and we were both equally invested.

Mark and I took Doodle and my little cousin Timothy, Doodle's new cousin and playmate, to Atlantic City on a bus trip. It was a precious experience. We started in the casino, where we ate and enjoyed the live musical entertainment. The artists were great. They allowed us to participate and get on stage while we sang "My Girl" and other classics. After the babies tired with their debut and live performances, we found our way to the boardwalk, where they played in the arcade for over an hour; finally we made it to the beach. We spent most of our day on the beach soaking up the sunrays while watching the boys swim freely in the water. They challenged the waves while we took their pictures. The trip was a great success. The casino allowed children to tour the common area in the same arena with the adults, and restricted them to travel only on the marble floors but not on the carpeted floors. It was there that I won $250 on twenty-one (blackjack), and Mark won $120 on the slot machines. That week Terry, Mark, and I decided to purchase Doodle a new video game system, the Xbox 360, with a couple of games, and he was elated and excited.

The following month Aunt Pat, Aunt Debbie, Mark, and I planned a trip to New York. We drove up state and stayed the weekend so that Patrick (Doodle's other cousin) and Doodle could bond with my dad, Anthony Sr. Doodle and his granddad hit it off very well. The trip was eventful and fun for everyone, I was glad everyone enjoyed themselves. Aunt Debbie and Aunt Pat developed a special bond with Doodle there. Time seemed to pass so fast that before I knew it, the summer was coming to an end and Christmas was approaching.

Time passed quickly, and Doodle was becoming acclimated to his new surroundings. We wanted Christmas to be special for him, so we asked him what he wanted well in advance. He said that he only wanted a few games to play on his Xbox 360. Since he kept his wish list to a minimum, I wanted to totally spoil him. Mark and I went all out to reward his good behavior. We had a Christmas dinner and shopped until we dropped.

As time passed the Department of Social Services had many request and hurdles to clear before we could complete this process of hopefully making Doodle our adopted child and not just our foster son. But even after all this time, he remains our foster son. However I feel in spite of what the paper says he is ours and a part of our family now and until the end of time. I promised myself I would fight for him and do everything in my power to protect, care, and, more importantly, love him as if he were born and raised since birth with Mark and me. Now we have a heavy schedule to fulfill going to see Doodle's psychiatrist, his case worker, his social worker, his lawyer visits,

DSS lawyer's visits, dentist appointments, doctor appointments, school meetings…and the list goes on.

Doodle has a story that would pierce even the coldest man's heart; he struggles with ADHD and bipolar disorder, and has a medical list that would exhaust you on sight. Naturally his challenges become my tests. I feel it's our duty to minimize a child's stressors, install spirituality to strengthen their faith. We need to teach children the proper way to address, face and conquer their adversities in a healthy and effective manner. My Dew (Doodle) had to overcome physical and mental abuse. Need I mention his parents were both addicted to drugs and alcohol? His biological father was killed several months before Doodle entered my home. Doodle's dad was a racist and he was killed in a bar fight over racial remarks. Not long after that traumatic event took place, Doodle witnessed his mom's last expression of love for him. She attempted to overdose in the house with just her and Doodle alone, forcing Doodle to pursue the police and to become the reason she's here today.

He had to take on an adult role on more than one occasion and still not allow his circumstances to deprive him of his childhood. Even still, Doodle's mother's struggles make me respect and care for her, because I can tell she loves her children. Plus it's important to be mindful she didn't get into this alone but circumstances force her to deal with life and her children alone. My guess is that it is to a large degree epigenetic.

Doodle, Terry, Mark and I fulfill our moral obligations to arrange for Doodle to visit his mom, sisters, and brothers, but only when we are present. For the first two years, Doodle would not visit unless someone from our immediate family was present. Afraid he might not return he makes sure to stress the fact that he wants to stay here and spares no feelings when he expresses himself. Knowing that Doodle just lost his biological dad, his mother was still in the act of addiction, and his five siblings were awarded to the state and either placed in different homes and facilities or simply away from home building their own family. Doodles sister Kay and I grew close over time and she has been a consistent support system she helps me keep their family together in many ways and I appreciate her. Kay is a fairly young girl but she works hard and contributes all that she can, but above all she is present and now a new addition to my family as well.

His situation only confirmed to me once again how important it is to press on, be strong, and overcome adversity. I wish I could carry his burden for him, although I am aware that our walk helps define us, and with the proper love and guidance he will be fine. Now that I have a child added to my equation, giving up is not an option. I lead by example and teach him by my actions.

Doodle is a survivor like me. I couldn't imagine being another disappointment in his life. He is a blessing to me, and it wasn't long after we began caring for him that more blessings came my way.

After two years of caring for my son Doodle, I was called by one of my elite best friends, Tee and her lover Kelly. They phoned because they were having severe problems with their son Jay. The state and the Juvenile Department were involved and in the process of taking custody of Jay from his biological mother Kelly. When Mark and I learned that our friends needed some support we didn't hesitate to visit them and have a family meeting with all parties evolved. I dropped everything because Tee is one of my very best friends, Jay is a good child with a promising future and I witnessed for myself that Kelly is a good person. I felt that Kelly was inexperienced with raising boys, young and lacked support and guidance in areas she needed support it most. With all things considered I concluded that she was a good mother with good intentions and that together with Tee filling the void they had a complete and positive family.

Before we closed our meeting we said a prayer and Kelly asked me if I could provide a place for Jay to stay. I told her to give me a day to speak to my mother, my son, and Mark. More importantly, I needed to pray about it and get back to her. I considered what effect this would have on my son Doodle, I talked to my family and consoled with my GOD. I decided to advise her to send him with his grandmother and get his father involved and if my suggestion doesn't work, I'll do what I can. At the time I was convinced it was best for him to reside with me, and my family was in support of him staying.

Sorry to say I wasn't sure if that was best for my family. Unfortunately Kelly's mom didn't take him. He stayed with a friend of Kelly's for thirty days and that made matters worse for Kelly and Jay. It was as if Jay was in the skillet and jumped out and into the fire. I was watching from a far and when Kelly confirmed what I already knew to be true; that matters had gotten worse and now she had no more resources, I then committed to being responsible for Jay. I really wanted to make this decision the very last option, because I am well aware that Kelly and I have come from two very different upbringings. That in turn would surely make matters concerning Jay very difficult for me. I'm well aware that I would have to deprogram Jay and teach him a whole new way of living. Just the move from the city to the county was a major adjustment alone.

Within a week Mark and I had this boy settled in the house, registered in Baltimore County public schools, and attending therapy for his indiscretions. We went to every court hearing and in the end we were appointed his legal guardians. We transferred apartments and upgraded to a three-bedroom apartment home. With this agreement his biological mom made a financial commitment with me that was painfully unsuccessful. We had a written contract that was legally notarized in addition to the court documents. Eventually I was forced to apply for child support, which was little to nothing, but I did appreciate it, because it was more than the hundred and fifty dollars a month that his mom and I originally agreed on. The situation created a lot of stress but I was determined to prevent this transition from damaging me and Tee's friendship, because she is more than a friend she is my family.

I was certain I could protect my friendship and still care for Jay. Giving up on him has never been an option. He has moved in and adjusted very well, he is an honor roll student and works hard to be a responsible young man. My sons Doodle and Jay get along very well and I'm pleased to be able to raise them as siblings. Knowing they both come from large immediate families make the adjusting process easier. Both my boys respect and love Mark and that's very important to me that everyone in my home is comfortable. My boys get along well with me and Mark's extended family on all sides. They relate to and show my grandmothers and Marks mom love and respect like biological family members. That alone is enough to make my heart just skip a beat. It feels so good to witness the people that I love and respect most, bound well with my kids.

When I look back, I realize it's been many years and time is moving quickly. I recognize that with the support of my mother and my grandmothers is what helps make my priorities doable. Taking care of my children, being attentive to my husb-wife, working, and achieving my goals have become my first priority while remembering to keep GOD up front. Even with the day-to-day situations you encounter on a job, in school or sometimes in your own home. You have to still push through the storm and don't let anything deter you from what you want to achieve.

What drives me is my love for what I do and my family. My family keeps me grounded. Knowing that I have others depending on me, makes me do what I have to do in order to get where I want to be. The reality is everyone makes mistakes, but it's obvious that my boy's biological mothers did do a lot of things right by them because they are truly both wonderful young men. I am thankful they love them enough to share them with us so together we can all assist them in feeling safe and loved on their journey to a successful future.

To further assist me in achieving my goals, I applied for a class in phlebotomy and was determined to complete the course. I strongly desired moving into a new field because "a man with one option has no option." The class was new and educational. Completing the course has allowed me to become a certified phlebotomist. More importantly, it has taught my children to set goals and complete them. Be a success, and define your own future.

Through this journey from within, I have now learned to look for what I can offer to the world, instead of what I can get from it. I believe that I can make a difference just by being a positive person and sharing my truth. I think everyone wants to do what is right and I share that desire. But now I want to do what is right for a more meaningful reason, not just because it is the right thing to do. I want to actually be a part of making this world a better place. Satan tries to make us believe that *giving up* is the easy thing to do, but the truth is *giving up is so hard to do*!

I am Anthony Leslie Jr., and this is *my truth*, and this is *My Journey from Within*!

Chocolate Arabian Prince, White Chocolate,
Rabbit and Ant-Moe out on the town

Terry and Tony at a function for the children

Terry and Mark supporting our babies

CHAPTER 11

Food For Thought
From The Best Book Ever, The Bible

<u>2 Timothy 3: 7</u>—Always learning and yet never able to come to an accurate knowledge of truth.

<u>2 Timothy 3: 16</u>—All scripture is inspired of GOD and beneficial for teaching, for reproving, for setting things straight, for disciplining in righteousness.

<u>Psalms 83: 18</u>—People may know that you, whose name is Jehovah. You alone are the most High over all the earth.

<u>Exodus 6: 2-3</u>—And GOD went on to speak to Moses and to say to him: "I am Jehovah." And I used to appear to Abraham, Isaac, and Jacob as GOD Almighty but as respects my name Jehovah I did not make myself known to them.

<u>Matthew 3: 16-17</u>—After being baptized Jesus immediately came up from the water; and look! The heavens were opened up, and he saw descending like a dove GOD's spirit coming upon him. Look! Also there was a voice from the heavens that said: "This is my Son, the beloved, whom I have approved."

<u>Matthew 4: 3-4, & 7</u>—Satan came and said to Jesus: "If you are son of GOD, tell these stones to become loaves of bread." But in reply Jesus said: "It is written, 'Man must live, not on bread alone, but on every utterance coming forth through Jehovah's mouth." Jesus said to him: "Again it is written, 'You must not put Jehovah your GOD to the test.'"

<u>John 3: 16</u>—For GOD loved the world so much that he gave his only begotten son, in order that everyone exercising faith in him might not be destroyed but have everlasting life.

<u>Romans 12: 17-21</u>—Return evil for evil to no one. Provide fine things in the sight of all men. If possible, as far as it depends upon you, be peaceable with all men. Do not avenge yourselves, beloved, but yield place to wrath; for it is written: "Vengeance is mine; I will repay, says GOD." But "If your enemy is hungry, feed him; if he is thirsty, give him something to drink; for by doing this you will heap fiery coals upon his head" Do not let yourself be conquered by the evil but keep conquering the evil with good.

<u>Matthew 7: 1-5</u> — Stop judging that you may not be judged; for with what judgment you are judging, you will be judged; and with the measure that you are measuring out, they will measure out to you. Why, then do you look at the straw in your brother's eye, but do not consider the rafter in your own eye? Or how can you say to your brother, Allow me to extract the straw from your eye; when, look! A rafter is in your own eye? Hypocrite! First extract the rafter from your own eye, and then you will see clearly how to extract the straw from your brother's eye.

<u>1st Kings 8: 46-50</u> —If they sin against you (for there is no man who does not sin) and you are angry with them and deliver them to the enemy, so that they are carried away captive to the enemy's land, far or near; Yet if they think and consider in the land where they were carried captive, and repent and make supplication to you there, saying, we have sinned and have done perversely and wickedly; If they repent and turn to you with all their mind and with all their heart in the land of their enemies who took them captive, and pray to you toward their land which you gave to their fathers, the city which you have chosen, and the house I have built for your name. Then hear their prayers and their supplication in heaven, your dwelling place, and

defend their cause and maintain their right. And forgive your people, who have sinned against you, and grant them compassion before those who took them captive, that they may have pity and be merciful to them.

Matthew 7: 7-8 —"Keep on asking, and it will be given you; Keep on seeking, and you will find; Keep on knocking, and it will be opened to you. For everyone asking receives, and everyone seeking finds, and to everyone knocking it will be opened".

Matthew 7: 12-14 —"All things, therefore, that you want men to do to you, you must also likewise do to them; this in fact, is what the Law and the prophets mean". Go in through the narrow gate; because broad and spacious is the road leading off into destruction, and many are the ones going through it; whereas narrow is the gate and cramped is the road leading off into life, and few are the ones finding it".

Matthew 7: 28-29— Now when Jesus finished these sayings, the effect was that the crowds were astounded at his way of teaching; for he was teaching them as a person having authorities, and not as their scribes.

Matthew 10: 29-31— Do not two sparrows sell for a coin of small value? Yet not one of them will fall to the ground without your Father's [Knowledge]. But the very hairs of your head are numbered. Therefore have no fear: you are worth more than many sparrows.

2ⁿᵈ Corinthians 8: 12-15— For if the readiness is there first, it is especially acceptable according to what a person has, not according to what a person does not have. For I do not mean for it to be easy for others, but hard on you; but that by means of an equalizing your surplus just now might offset their deficiency, in order that their surplus might also offset your deficiency, that an equalizing might take place. Just as it is written: "The person with much did not have too much, and the person with little did not have too little."

1ˢᵗ Kings 8: 46—If they sin against you [for there is no man who does not sin] and you are angry with them and deliver them to the enemy, so that they are carried away captive to the enemy's land, far or near.

1ˢᵗ Kings 8: 50—And forgive your people, who have sinned against you, and all their transgressions against you, and grant them compassion before those who took them captive, that they may have pity and be merciful to them.

Isaiah 46: 5-7— "To whom will you liken me or make me equal or compare me, that we may resemble each other?" They lavish gold out of the cup or bag, weigh out silver on the scales, and hire a goldsmith, and he fashions it into a GOD; then they fall down yes, they worship it! They bear it upon their shoulders [in religious processions or into battle]; they carry it and set it down in its place, and there it stands. It cannot move from its place. Even if one cries to it for help, yet [the idol] cannot answer or save him out of his distress.

Psalms 51: 5—Behold, I was brought forth in [a state of] iniquity; my mother was sinful who conceived me [and I too am sinful].

Romans 5: 12—That is why, just as through one man sin entered into the world and death through sin, and thus death spread to all men because they had all sinned.

1ˢᵗ Peter 5: 8-11— Keep your senses, be watchful. Your adversary, the Devil, walks about like a roaring lion, seeking to devour [someone]. After you suffered a little while, the GOD of all undeserved kindness, who called you to his everlasting glory in union with Christ, will himself finish your training, he will make you strong. To him be the might forever Amen.

Ecclesiastes 3: 7-8—For everything there is an appointed time, a time to rip apart and a time to sew together, a time to love and a time to hate; a time for war and a time for peace.

Romans 8: 31—What, then shall we say to these things? If GOD is for us, who will be against us?

Isaiah 41: 10-13—Do not be afraid, for I am with you. Do not gaze about, for I am your GOD. I will fortify you. I will really help you. I will really keep fast hold of you with my right hand of righteousness. "Look!" All those getting heated up against you will become ashamed and be humiliated. The men in a quarrel with you will become as nothing and will perish. You will search for them, but you will not find them, those men in a struggle with you. They will become as something nonexistent and as nothing, those men at war with you. For I, Jehovah your GOD, am grasping your right hand, the one saying to you, 'Do not be afraid. I myself will help you.'

Hebrews 4: 12–13—For the word of GOD is alive and exerts power and is sharper than any two-edged sword and pierces even to the dividing of soul and spirit and of joints and their marrow, and is able to discern thoughts and intentions of the heart. And there is not a creation that is not manifest to sight, but all things are naked and openly exposed to the eyes of him with whom we have an accounting.

Hebrews 8: 11—And they will by no means teach each one his fellow citizen and each one his brother, saying: "Know Jehovah! For they will all know me, from the least one to the greatest one of the least one of them. For I shall be merciful to their unrighteous deeds, and I shall by no means call their sins to mind anymore."

<u>Acts 2: 38</u>—Peter said to them: "Repent, and let each one of you be baptized in the name of Jesus Christ for forgiveness of your sins, and you will receive the free gift of the holy spirit."

<u>Jeremiah 31: 34</u>—And they will no more teach each one his companion and each his brother, saying, "Know Jehovah!" for they will all of them even to the greatest one of them, is the utterance of Jehovah. "For I shall forgive their error, and their sin *I shall remember no more.*" (Italics are mine.)

<u>James 5: 15</u>—And the prayer of faith will make the indisposed one well, and GOD will rise him up. Also if he has committed sins it will be forgiven him.

<u>James 5: 19-20</u>—My brother, if anyone among you is misled from the truth and another turns him back, know that he who turns a sinner back from the error of his way will save his soul from death and will cover a multitude of sins.

<u>1 John 5: 17, 20-21</u>—All unrighteousness is sin; and yet there is a sin that does not incur death. But we know that the Son of GOD has come, and he has given us intellectual capacity that we may gain the knowledge of the true one. And we are in union with the true one, by means of his Son Jesus Christ. This is the true GOD and life everlasting. Little children, guard yourselves from **idols**.

<u>1ˢᵗ Corinthians 8: 5-7</u>— For even though there are those who are called "gods," whether in heaven or on earth, just as there are many "gods" and many "lords" there is actually to us one GOD the Father, out of whom all things are, and we for him; and there is one LORD, Jesus Christ, through whom all things are, and we for him. Nevertheless, there is not this knowledge in all persons; but some, being accustomed until now to the idol, eat food as something sacrificed to an idol, and their conscience, being weak, is defiled.

<u>Jonah 2: 8-9</u>—As for those who are observing the idols of untruth, they leave their own loving-kindness. But as for me, with the voice of thanksgiving I will sacrifice to you. What I have vowed, I will pay. Salvation belongs to GOD

<u>Joshua 1: 9</u>—Have I not commanded you? Be courageous and strong. Do not suffer shock or be terrified, for Jehovah your GOD is with you wherever you go.

These Scriptures weigh heavy on my heart. The words have depth and encourage me to try to behave like a Christian. People may wonder why a born sinner, such as me believes and depends strongly on the Holy Scriptures. It's only because no sin is greater than any other sin. I am worthy to speak to and about the GOD of my understanding, freely and without judgment. I honestly shared my *Naked Truth* [Uncensored] with people in hopes of touching someone who can relate, or simply to encouraging someone who feels hopeless. I'm convinced I have been forgiven, and I can recognize my growth. Embracing my past, sharing my truth, asking for forgiveness and also being able to forgive has helped me heal deep rooted wounds. Covering up and being ashamed only makes setback possible. Please don't be ashamed of your past, because we all have one. Remember we are all children of GOD and made in his image. You can refer to him as Allah, Jesus, Jehovah, The Messiah, or just GOD, etc. But if you are sincere, he will hear you because GOD is LOVE and he is the only one who can read our hearts and minds. GOD knows you better than you know yourself. His eyes are always on the sparrow **Matthew 10: 29-31** [Refer to chapter 11], and if he loves and watches every small ordinary sparrow, imagine how you hold his interest. Imagine what you can do or what he will carry you through with great success if you simply welcome him into your heart and put ALL your faith in GOD. As GOD fearing people we must be able to decrease in order to allow GOD to grant a increase in our lives.

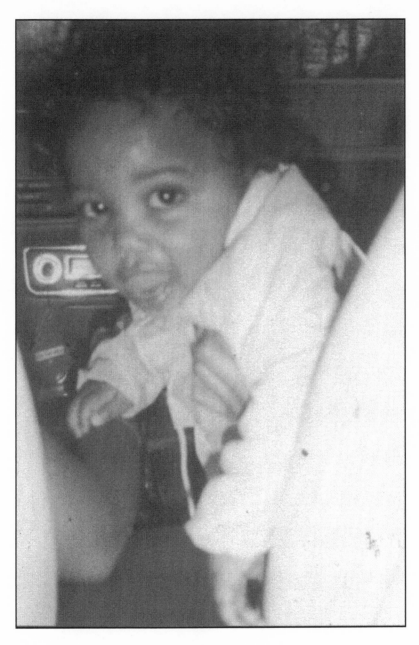

Anthony L. Leslie Jr.
Fatty

My Great Grandmother Dorothy Ghee RIP

My Grand Father Avon Mac RIP

Maternal Grandmother and my only 1st female cousin

Barbara H Snell and Michael H Snell-
R.I.P.

Mike is my biological cousin that my grandmother adopted from her sister and made Michael known to me as my uncle but above all he is my friend

Barbara Snell (Mommy), Tamara Snell-
(Tammy), and Anthony Leslie Jr. (Tony)

Paternal Grandmother and my only 1st male cousin

Arnold Pop-pop Pig-(R.I.P.) and Marilyn Leslie Dee-Jay Granny

Marilyn Leslie (Granny), Ronald Leslie (Bubby)
and Anthony Leslie Jr. (Fatty)

Terry Snell, Monique Ghee, Tony Leslie Jr., and
Barbara Snell @ the family reunion

Mark Gentry, Terry Snell, Monique Ghee, Tony Leslie Jr., Barbara Snell

Adrian L-Chatman my 1st cousin and Tony
Living @ grannies during my addiction.
Thanks Cousin for loving me uninterrupted and genuinely until I was in
a position to Love myself you are and will always be my sister-friend!

Adrian and Tony celebrating my graduation from
high school @ Corinthians Lounge 21 & older

Octavia Yoddy Leslie (Aunt) and Mark Gentry (Husb-Wife)

My Family Patricia L, Ronald L, Angela L, Courtney
S, Shetia L, Deborah D, Mark G, Terry S, Anthony L,
Doritha L, and Friend to the family Colton

Queen Annie Leslie, Robert, Anthony, and
Terry having a snowball fight

Terry (Tee), Mark (Rabbit), Robbie (Dew), Tony, Queen (Pudd)

Terry and Robert @ the racecar wet-track

Tony Leslie Jr. @ the grand Go-Cart dual Racetrack

Robert (Robbie), Mark (Markie) and Timothy
(Brucie) @ the Arcade on the boardwalk in
Atlantic City

Mark, Timmy, Tony and Robert at the
Taj Mahal Casino in Atlantic City

Tony, Robbie, Justin, and Mark @ the Christian
based River Valley Ranch and Horse Park

Robert W, Tony H, Tony L, Mark G, Paul,
Wayne G, and Paul @ My friends
Wayne and Tony H house

Robert, Tony and Queen Annie

Doodle, Tony, & Kaviah @ the Inner Harbor

Mark, and Tony @ one of our Best friend Latasha's Party

Tony Leslie Jr. Carla Johnson and Cori Johnson (Niece in laws/Friends)

Mark, Terry and Queen Annie @ 31 Flavors

Me my crew and my pit Killer

Tiffany Mark, Robbie Tony Justin and Queen
Annie on our way to get married

Tiffeny Anthony and Keyonna my second cousins

Me and the boys

Mark

Anthony

Mark Anthony

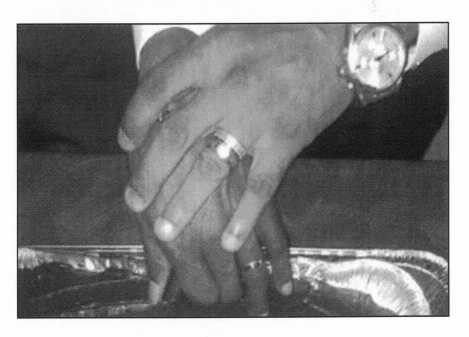

August 16, 2013
A Historic Moment
Mark-Anthony's Wedding Day

Acknowledgements

-This one's dedicated to the GOD of my understanding. You are truly my rock and savior. You are always on time, and your presence speaks volumes. If we could only take time to notice you, our lives would be meaningful and have purpose. Thanks for loving me as I am and loaning me to my mom, because before anything, I am truly a child of GOD.

-2 my mom, Terry. Thanks 4 all the roles you fulfill. You are truly my very best friend, my mentor, my daughter, my disciplinarian, my protector, & my prayer warrior. I know it's because of your constant prayers coupled w/ others that I'm here today. You make life in this chaotic world make sense. I'm proud 2 be your one & only child, because I'm the only thug in the hood that is wild enough 2 tame you (Eve). Thanks 4 listening & teaching me how 2 survive. You are truly my very first LOVE. You have my Love and eternal friendship.

-2 my husb-wife, Mark Gentry. Only GOD knows the asset you are. Thanks 4 the thirteen years you put in. I am forever in your debt. Thanks 4 taking notice & encouraging me 2 shine & seize the moment. You will 4ever be My Stinky. I love you 2 life & when this life is over, I'll wait 4 you 2 meet me on the moon. (Phyllis Hyman)

-My son Robert, no matter how old you get, you will 4ever be my baby boy. Remember w/ prayer, faith, & hard work you can achieve anything. Ur presence is proof that GOD answers prayers.

-Queen Annie, you are my 1ˢᵗ baby & you always project love & bring me joy.

-2 my grandmother Barbara, my true soul mate. What can I say? You introduced me to Jehovah GOD & taught me 2 send all my prayers through his son, Jesus Christ. You above all are a fine example of a Christian woman. Thanks 4 teaching me the value of friendship. MY CUP RUNNETH OVER.

-2 my grandmother Marilyn Leslie, thanks 4 being dad 4 all these years. You taught me 2 appreciate life & the cards I was dealt. Thank you 4 all your love & support. Words could never express my appreciation 4 caring 4 me as I am & carrying my pain. Thanks 4 the balance you display every day. You are truly a gift from GOD. I'm certain that when our days here on Earth ends, we will dance 2gether again in heaven. There are no cut cards w/ you, & your one friend I can share anything with.

-2 Clearance Pop-pop & Ms. Nora, thanks 4 showing us how a real man conducts himself. You are the youngest great-granddad ever, & I'm glad you are mine. I love you.

-Dorothy Ghee Momma, you could never be duplicated. Thank you 4 the graduation party. I'm so glad you got 2 see me graduate. I miss you (RIP).

-Arnold Pig, I miss you, pop-pop (RIP).

-My father, Anthony Sr., without you there would be no me. Even though you are miles away, I carry you in my prayers & in my heart. Prayer heals wounds, & prayers will bring you home soon.

-My stepdad & friend, Anthony/Frog, you gave me all the tools & support a child could ever ask 4. Thanks 4 sharing yourself and your family w/ me. I don't think I ever told you, you are a great person and a wonderful dad. I'm waiting 4 our next sit down.

-Brenda Barnes my step-grandmother & friend, you are a strong & real person, & I admire you. Thanks 4 accepting me as your grandson & taking good care of me. I will always love you. (Whitney Houston)

-My step-cousins Tee & Brandon Barnes we are thicker than blood.

-Thanks 2 my mother-in-law, Phyllis Gentry. You are a true blessing 2 me, & I greatly appreciate your unconditional Love & support.

-Ronald Leslie, thank you 4 always being not just my cousin & brother, but Thanks 4being a real friend. I love you 2 life.

-Reykia Leslie, my 1ˢᵗ cousin, you are 1 of my best friends & my sister. Nothing but death can keep me from you (color purple). Thanks 4 being a good example, & thanks 4 the unconditional love. You are me, & I am you.

-Tiffney Stoffa, my cousin & friend, life is not measured by what you have but what you give. Continue 2 give, & more will be revealed. Thanks 4 the support & encouragement, my partner in crime.

-My 1ˢᵗ cousin Tamara Snell it's only you & me on our side of the family, & you promised me your 1st son would be named after me, & Ur running out of time. (Ha-ha!)

-My cousins-in-law & my road dog, Carla, Cori, Chip, Karen & Joey Johnson Baby you give good love (Whitney Houston).

-Cathy BOO Gentry, my sister-in-law, you have been heaven-sent & a fine example of a true Christian woman.

-Cousin-in-law & my friends, John Lemon and Derrick Roberson, it's a rare thing 2 share an addiction & still remain friends in recovery (GOD is always working). Love ya 2 life.

-Toni Gentry you are my friend (Patti L), & I Love you.

-Uncle Gregory Howard, David Howard, Ronald Ghee, Dwayne Leslie & Preston Leslie, thank you 4 never judging me & always treating me like your own son. Thanks 4 always being there 4 me & my mom & playing dad at times.

-My Uncles Kenny Ivey, André Ghee, Rusty Ghee, Harry Ghee, Wendell H., Donald P., Gordon S. (RIP), Maxwell L. (RIP), & Lorenzo Howard (RIP), you will always hold a special place in my heart.

-My uncle & friend, Michael Howard (RIP), thanks 4 allowing me 2 help you. Helping you & loving you helped me more than anyone can ever imagine. Even though you couldn't speak, you always made me feel loved & appreciated. Thanks 4 helping me grow 2 be a kind & loving, responsible man. Thanks 4 teaching me how 2 speak w/ my actions, my eyes, & my heart.

-My Aunt Octavia Yoddy Leslie, you are special not only 2 your mom but 2 me as well. Thanks 4 treating me as your own. I will always be here 2 care 4 you.

-Godfather Charles Parker even though you are a reserved man with little words you played an important role in my life and I will never 4get you. Even though I'm grown now doesn't mean I don't still need you and your encouragement, SO STOP SLACKING! It meant the world to me to learn you took my kids to Dru Hill Park. I don't trust many people with my boys but you are greatly appreciated let's keep this pattern alive.

-My aunts Myrtice Howard, Cindy Ghee, Janet Howard, Carolyn Howard, Elsie Howard, Markida Barnes, Judith Howard, Bunny, Muriel & Debby Dorsey, Sunday Leslie, Pat & Linda Gunther, Rita Wells, & Lorrain Howard, it takes a village 2 raise a child, & I greatly appreciate you.

-My cousin & friend to the end, Adriane Chatmen Lemon Leslie, no matter how many miles life puts between us, I'm still just a phone call away. I will always carry you close 2 my heart. You helped me & didn't look down on me 4 almost a year when I was in my addiction, & I will never 4get it. I am so proud of you & how far you've come. Remember the race is not given 2 the swift but 2 he who burns the longest.

-Cousin Karen Howard, you have always been a joy to live with. I love and appreciate you.

-Cousin Courtney Smith, even though we roll heavy & hard, you will always be my Lama-Lamb, & I Love you 2 life, and thanks for being my model.

-Cousin Shetia Lee-Williams, life is a gift from GOD, what you do w/ it is your gift 2 GOD. I Love you, but GOD loves you more. Remember when everyone is absent, he's always there and I trust you in his care.

-Cousin Keyonna East, we had our run & that's a book all by itself. You will always be my lil' sister.

-Cousin Kiyenna Nelson, you are really a female me and I love you kiddo.

-Cousin Monique Ghee, I've always loved Josephine Baker, but I never thought I was related 2 her. Thanks 4 being my cousin & friend.

-My brother Randy Sellers, I Love you more and more everyday. (I can honestly say I AM REALLY PROUD OF YOU, you are the best brother from another mother)

-My sisters Georgia & Donna, I love you girls.

-My close cousins Sharon Bowie, Tevin Howard, Rusty Ghee Jr., Deshawn Leslie (RIP), Michael Seaborne, Edward Sparrow, Daniel B, Patrick S, Marcia Saunders, Tavory T, Tyrone Rawls Sr, Tyrone Rawls Jr., Brittney Rawls, Myla Ghee, Kyla Ghee, Jamie Howard, Raymond Jackson, Jason Ghee, Cori Harvey, John Harvey, Dottie Harvey, Sharon Howard, Monica Jackson, Jamie Brown, Portia Jackson, Devin W, Douglas M, Danielle Howard, Morgan & Megan Parker, Ashley H., Doggie H Jr., & Chris H., and Amanda Sparrow, I am proud of you, I'm proud 2 call you family, & above all I'm proud 2 say 2 ya'll I LOVE you.

-Cousin Earl H and your beautiful family, I always admired the commitment and dedication you displayed toward your children.

-Dorian Vaughn & Kayvieah Butler, you will always be a part of me, & I will always be here 4 you. Thanks 4 being the ideal duel. It was a pleasure taking a part in raising you.

-Lil' Ronnie & Patrick, I Love you boys so much.

-My godson, Jordan Anthony Lemon, you have been blessed in more ways than you could ever imagine. I love you lil' man.

-2 my dear friends Melanie S & Nigel B & the kids, Sean, Danielle and Vaughn, I love & miss you all.

-My best friend Tiffany (Marilyn M) & Latasha (2-Pac) Saunders & my second family, I could not have handpicked a better best friend & sister 4 all the tea in china. I love you, girl. I promise our business is my next priority, right after me and Stinky tie the knot. Floom you have my love and eternal friendship.

-Ebony Flemming Leslie, I love you.

-Baby sugar, you piece of Courtney & Devin.

-Cousin Latoya (TOAT)Barbour Thanks for helping me lay it down at the PROM, you have never changed since we were small children and I Love you Kiddo

-My girl Shuron Rhodes & Max, I love you.

-My brothers in the LIFE and my true friends Wayne Gabbert and Tony Harvard, I love and appreciate you. You could visit us 4 a change!!!

-Aunt Dora Leslie, we walk the streets 2 the church & GOD blessed you, so continue 2 praise him. I Love you. Thanks 4 always giving me yourself.

-2 Israel Cason my friend and teacher and the I CAN'T WE CAN PROGRAM thanks for the love & support.

-Aunt/Uncle Kat Angela Leslie, you are the perfect package, & if u weren't my aunt, I would marry you. You have always been strong independent & a lady 1st & I love that. Thanks 4 always keeping it real w/ me & thanks 4 being a fine example for me and all my cousins.

-My aunt Patricia Leslie, the world may never know or ever understand things as only you & I do. Remember: GOD, self, & then everything else.

-My best friend Nakia Lewis, I love you & your family more than you'll ever know. I always see GOD in you. Thanks 4 sharing your light, insight, love, & prayers. Some things I couldn't share, but I imagined you saying, "I love you just the same."

-Manny slick where you @ bae'

-Superfriends remember always keep GOD up front and be blessed

-All my classmates & co-workers and distant friends thank you for the history and good laughs

-Zenobia Clark & family, my stylist & friends, thanks 4 the magic you work on my mane. Continue 2 give Jehovah all the praise.

-Jay Wilson, they say no news is good news. When I see you, I'm going 2 send you 2 drop, then pull my foot out your a**. I love you, man. (ICWC)

-Stacey Gilbert I love you and really appreciate our friendship thanks for always being there.

-My friend Kay-Kay Anderson I love you for you and thanks for being a real friend in school at home and now. Thanks for a wonderful prom and for being my model

-Tia and Jessie R my real Safeway crew I love and appreciate you more than you'll ever know!!!!!!!!!!!!!!!!!!!!!!

-Vikki from Safeway I Love ya baby

-Anjye Herrera, my girl and my faithful co-worker, the sky is the limit.

-Anyone I fought (I'm sorry) for losing control, I hope u forgive me and recognize the role you played, if not cool, just keep living, but know that I am sorry!

-Special thanks 2 my pastor & friend, Walter Whitaker, & the Whitaker family. Thank you 4 all that you give and the blessings you share. I Love you, & I believe in what you are doing. Thank you 4 always accepting me & my family. Real recognizes real, & you are as real as it gets. When my friends need help & their problems are out of my reach, I can count on you 2 bring the word. You truly save lives, & you are greatly appreciated.

-Special thanks 2 my BROTHERS in THE TRUTH, Anthony/Frog B, Glenn W., Michael P., & Kevin W. Thank you 4 your hard work & time you shared with me and my boys studying the Bible. I know I'm a work in progress, but your actions speak volumes, & you give me the greatest gift man can give: the WORD OF GOD.

-Whitney Houston, Phyllis Hyman, Biggie, Luther Vandross, Michael Jackson, and Donnie Hathaway, your talent is still unmatched and I thank you for unselfishly sharing yourself and your talent with me and the world RIP

-Lil' Kim the Queen BEE thanks for the inspiration, After changing the title many times all it took was a Queen Bee movement! I SALUTE YOU.

-2 my celebrity friends in my mind, I got nuttin' but love for ya baby & I look forward 2 working with you in the near future; Whoopi Goldberg, Steve Harvey, Ellen DeGeneres, Oprah W, Tyler Perry, Drew Barry More, Queen Latifah, John singleton, Ving Rhames, Forrest Whitaker, Herbert Ross, Tony Kayeand, and John Morrissey,

-The people that was a good influence & was a fine example with being a Guardian & Foster parent:

-Grandmother Barbara Snell thanks for loving and caring for my Uncle   Michael

-Aunt Judith Howard you are simply the best and GOD has blessing lined up just 4 you

-Mr. & Mrs. Richardson thanks for being a good example! Raymond Richard you are loved and missed (RIP).

-Aunt Debbie Dorsey you are a great mother and a wonderful friend

-Special thanks 2 Letta Moore, Leroy Mckenzie and the Create Space team. I appreciate your constructive criticism & praise. Without Your encouragement & support, I couldn't imagine completing this process. I hope ya'll are ready 4 round 2 It was great working you.

-Special thanks to anyone who bought, read or supports me and my books, Thanks for the feedback and emails. I can't thank you enough and I appreciate each of you. I won't forget you-all of whom make me better than I am.

—Anthony L. Leslie Jr.

Made in the USA
Charleston, SC
14 January 2014